FIGURE DRAWING
FOR ALL IT'S WORTH

ALSO BY ANDREW LOOMIS:

FUN WITH A PENCIL

CREATIVE ILLUSTRATION

SUCCESSFUL DRAWING

FIGURE DRAWING
FOR ALL IT'S WORTH

ANDREW LOOMIS

Figure Drawing For All It's Worth

ISBN: 9780857680983

Published by
Titan Books
A division of Titan Publishing Group Ltd.
144 Southwark St.
London
SE1 0UP

This edition: May 2011
16

To receive advance information, news, competitions, and exclusive offers online, please sign up for the Titan newsletter on our website: **www.titanbooks.com**

Did you enjoy this book? We love to hear from our readers. Please e-mail us at: **readerfeedback@titanemail.com** or write to Reader Feedback at the above address.

A CIP catalogue record for this title is available from the British Library.

Printed and bound in China.

DEDICATION

TO THE YOUNG MEN AND WOMEN

OF THE UNITED STATES

WHO HAVE TURNED

TO THE DRAWING OF THE HUMAN FIGURE

AS A MEANS OF LIVELIHOOD,

THIS VOLUME IS

RESPECTFULLY DEDICATED

CONTENTS, INCLUDING ILLUSTRATIONS

CONTENTS, INCLUDING ILLUSTRATIONS

CONTENTS, INCLUDING ILLUSTRATIONS

CONTENTS, INCLUDING ILLUSTRATIONS

CONTENTS, INCLUDING ILLUSTRATIONS

CONTENTS, INCLUDING ILLUSTRATIONS

FIGURE DRAWING
FOR ALL IT'S WORTH

AN OPENING CHAT

DEAR READER:

For many years the need of a further book on the subject of figure drawing has been apparent to me. I have waited for such a book to appear which could be recommended to the many young artists with whom I have come in contact. Finally, I have come to the realization that such a book, regardless of one's ability as an author, could be written only by a man actually in the field of commercial art, who in his experience had met and countered with the actual problems that must be clarified. I recall how frantically, in the earlier days of my own experience, I searched for practical information that might lend a helping hand in making my work marketable. Being in the not unusual position of having to support myself, it was the predicament of having to make good at art or being forced to turn to something else.

Across this wide country there are many of you in that predicament. You, also possessed of that unaccountable urge which seemingly comes from nowhere, want to speak the language of art. You love to draw. You wish to draw well. If there is any chance, you greatly wish to make a living at it. Perhaps I can help you. I sincerely hope so, for I think I have lived through every minute you are now living. Perhaps I can compile some of the information that experience tells me you want and need. I do not pretend to undervalue the fine work that has been done; the difficulty has always been in finding it and sorting out what is of practical value and putting it into practice. I believe that the greater chances of success lie in the mental approach to the work, rather than in sheer technical knowledge, and since the mental approach has not often been stressed, here lies the opportunity to serve you.

I not only assume that my reader is interested in drawing but that he wishes from his toes up to become an efficient and self-supporting craftsman. I assume that the desire to express yourself with pen and pencil is not only urgent but almost undeniable, and that you feel you *must do something about it*. I feel that talent means little unless coupled with an insatiable desire to give an excellent personal demonstration of ability. I feel also that talent must be in company with a capacity for unlimited effort, which provides the power that eventually hurdles the difficulties that would frustrate lukewarm enthusiasm.

Let us try to define that quality which makes an artist "tick." Every bit of work he does starts out with the premise that it has a message, a purpose, a job to do. What is the most direct answer, the simplest interpretation of that message he can make? Stripping a subject to its barest and most efficient essentials is a mental procedure. Every inch of the surface of his work should be considered as to whether it bears important relationship to a whole purpose. He sees, and his picture tells us the importance of what he sees and how he feels about it. Then within his picture he stresses what is of greatest importance, and subordinates what must be there but is of lesser importance. He will place his area of greatest contrast about the head of the most important character. He will search diligently for means to make that character express the emotion in facial expression and pose that is to be the all important theme. He will first draw attention to that character, by every means available. In other words, he plans and thinks, and does not passively accept simply because it exists. Not far back in the annals of art the ability to achieve just a lifelike appearance might have caused some wonder in a spectator, enough to capture his interest. Today with color photography and the excellence of the camera going perhaps even further in that respect, we are surfeited with realism par excellence, until mere lifelike representation is not enough. There is no other course than somehow to go beyond obvious fact to pertinent fact, to characterization, to the emotional and dramatic, to selection and taste, to simplification, subordination, and accentuation. It is ten per cent how you draw, and ninety per cent *what you draw*. Equally defining everything within your picture area, in value, edge and detail, will add no more than can be achieved in photography. Subordination may be achieved by diffusion, by closeness of color and value to surrounding areas, by simplification of insistent detail, or by omission. Accentuation is achieved by the opposite in each case, by sharpness, contrast, detail, or any added device.

I take this opportunity to impress upon you, my reader, how important you really are in the whole of art procedure. You, your personality, your individuality come first. Your pictures are your by-product. Everything about your pictures is, and should be, a little of you. They will be a reflection of your knowledge, your experience, your observation, your likes and dislikes, your good taste, and your thinking. So the real concentration is centered on you, and your work follows along in the wake of what mental self-improvement you are making. It has taken me a lifetime to realize that. So before we talk at all about drawing, it is important to sell you strongly on yourself, to plant that urge so definitely in your consciousness that you must know at once that most of it comes from the other end of your pencil rather than the business end.

As a student I thought there was a formula of some kind that I would get hold of somewhere, and thereby become an artist. There is a formula, but it has not been in books. It is really plain old courage, standing on one's own feet,

and forever seeking enlightenment; courage to develop your way, but learning from the other fellow; experimentation with your own ideas, observing for yourself, a rigid discipline of doing over that which you can improve. I have never found a book that stressed the importance of myself as the caretaker of my ability, of staying healthy mentally and physically, or that gave me an inkling that my courage might be strained to the utmost. Perhaps that is not the way to write books, but I can see no harm in the author realizing that he is dealing with personalities, and that there is something more important than technique. In art we are dealing with something far removed from a cold science, where the human element is everything. At least I am determined to established a fellowship with my reader, welcoming him to the craft at which I have spent so many years. If I have any blue chips I can pass on to him, I lay them before him so that he may join in the game. I cannot profess to know more than the experience of one individual. However, one individual experience if wide enough might well cover many of the problems that will doubtless come to others. Solutions of those problems may provide like solutions. I can lay out an assortment of facts and fundamentals that were helpful to me. I can speak of the idealizations, the practical hints and devices that will undoubtedly make drawings more salable. Since the requirements are almost universal, and since my own experience does not vary greatly from the average experience of my contemporaries, I offer my material without setting up myself and my work as a criterion. In fact, I would prefer, if it were possible, to subordinate my own viewpoint, or technical approach, and leave the reader as free as possible for individual decision and self-expression. I use my experience merely to clarify the general requirements.

It should be obvious that, first of all, salable

figure drawing must be good drawing, and "good drawing" means a great deal more to the professional than to the beginner. It means that a figure must be convincing and appealing at the same time. It must be of idealistic rather than literal or normal proportion. It must be related in perspective to a constant eye level or viewpoint. The anatomy must be correct, whether exposed to the eye or concealed beneath drapery or costume. The light and shadow must be so handled as to impart a living quality. Its action or gesture, its dramatic quality, expression, and emotion must be convincing. Good drawing is neither an accident nor the result of an inspired moment when the Muses lend a guiding hand. Good drawing is a co-ordination of many factors, all understood and handled expertly, as in a delicate surgical operation. Let us say that each factor becomes an instrument or part of a *means of expression*. It is when the means of expression is developed as a whole that inspiration and individual feeling come into play. It is possible for anybody to be "off" at any time in any one or more of the factors. Every artist will do "good ones" and "bad ones." The bad will have to be thrown out and done over. The artist should, of course, make a critical analysis to determine why a drawing is bad; usually he will be forced to go back to fundamentals, for bad drawing springs from basic faults as surely as good drawing springs from basic merits.

Therefore a useful book of figure drawing cannot treat one phase alone, as the study of anatomy; it must also seek out and co-ordinate all the basic factors upon which good drawing depends. It must consider both aesthetics and sales possibilities, technical rendering and typical problems to be solved. Otherwise the reader is only partially informed; he is taught but one angle, and then left to flounder.

May I assume that you as a young artist are facing a bread-and-butter problem? Whenever you achieve sufficient technical ability, there will be an income waiting for you. From that point on your earnings will increase in ratio to your improvement. In the fields of practical art the ranks thin out at the top, just as they do everywhere else. There is not an advertising agency, a magazine publisher, a lithograph house, or an art dealer's that will not gladly open its doors to real ability that is new and different. It is mediocrity to which the door is closed. Unfortunately most of us are mediocre when we start out; by and large, most commercial artists of outstanding ability had no more than average talent at the start.

May I confess that two weeks after entering art school, I was advised to go back home? That experience has made me much more tolerant of an inauspicious beginning than I might otherwise have been, and it has given me additional incentive in teaching.

Individuality of expression is, without question, an artist's most valuable asset. You could make no more fatal error than to attempt to duplicate, for the sake of duplication alone, either my work or that of any other individual. Use another's style as a crutch only—until you can walk alone. Trends of popularity are as changeable as the weather. Anatomy, perspective, values remain constant; but you must diligently search for new ways to apply them. The greatest problem here is to provide you with a solid basis that will nurture individuality and not produce imitation. I grant that a certain amount of imitation in the earliest phase of learning may be necessary in order that self-expression may have an essential background. But there can be no progress in any art or craft without an accumulation of individual experience. The experience comes best through your own effort or observation, through self-instruction, the reading of a book, or the study of an old master. These experiences are bundled together to form your working knowledge, and the process should never stop. New, creative ideas are usually variants of the old.

In this volume I shall try to treat the figure as a living thing, its power of movement related to its structure and its movement separated into several kinds. We shall draw the nude for the purpose of better understanding the draped figure. We shall think of the figure as possessed of bulk and weight, as being exposed to light and therefore shadow, and hence set into space as we know it. Then we shall try to understand light for what it is; and how form, with its planes of various direction, is affected by it. We shall consider the head and its structure separately. In other words, we shall provide a foundation that will enable you to make your figures original and convincing. The interpretation, the type, the pose, the drama, the costume, and the accessories will all be yours. Whether your figures are drawn for an advertisement, to illustrate a story, or for a poster or a calendar will not change appreciably the fundamental demands upon your knowledge. Technique is not so important as the young artist is inclined to believe; the living and emotional qualities—the idealization you put into your work—are far more important. So are your selection and taste in costume and setting—provided you have mastered fundamentals. The smartest dress in the world will not be effective on a badly drawn figure. Expression or emotion cannot possibly be drawn into a face that is poorly constructed. You cannot paint in color successfully without some conception of light and color values, or even hope to build a composition of figures until you know how to draw them in absolute perspective. Your job is to glorify and idealize the everyday material about you.

It is my purpose from start to finish of this book to lend you a hand to the top of the hill, but upon reaching the crest to push you over and leave you to your own momentum. I have hired and paid the best models I could find, knowing that the limited funds of the average young artist, would not permit that. If you study my drawings in the light of a model posing for you, rather than thinking of them as something to be duplicated line for line and tone for tone, I think you will in the end derive greater benefit. With every page I suggest you place your pad at the side of the book. Try to get the meaning behind the drawing much more than the drawing itself. Keep your pencil as busy as possible. Try figures varying as much as possible from those in my pages. Set up figures roughly, from the imagination, make them do all sorts of actions. If it is possible to draw from the live model in school or elsewhere, do so by all means, utilizing as best you can the fundamentals we have here. If you can take photos or have access to them, try your skill in drawing from them, adding what idealization you think should be there.

It might be a good plan to read the entire book at the start so that you will better understand the general plan of procedure. Other kinds of drawing such as still life should be supplemented, for all form presents the general problem of contour, planes, light and shadow.

Get used to using a soft pencil, one that will give considerable range from light to dark. A thin, weak and gray drawing has practically no commercial value. The switching to a pen and black drawing ink is not only interesting but has real value commercially. Use one that is fairly flexible. Pull the pen to make your line, never push it at the paper, for it will only catch and splutter. Charcoal is a fine medium for study. A large tissue or layout pad is excellent to work on.

Perhaps the best way is to suggest that you use the book in whatever manner suits you best.

THE APPROACH TO FIGURE DRAWING

The first chapter of this book will be treated a little differently from the others, as a prelude to the actual figure, and to lay the groundwork of the structure we are later to build. This part of the book will be of especial value to the layout man and to the artist for the preparation of preliminary sketches, roughs, the setting down of ideas, suggestions of actions and pose, where the figure must be drawn without the use of models or copy. This is the sort of work the artist does in advance of the finished work. This, in other words, is the work with which he sells himself to the prospective client. In that respect it is most important since it really creates opportunity. He will be able to prepare this work intelligently so that when he gets to the final work he will not be confused with new problems of perspective, spacing, and other difficulties.

The reader is urged to give this chapter his utmost attention since it is unquestionably the most important chapter in the book, and one to pay good dividends for the concentrated effort involved.

I. THE APPROACH TO FIGURE DRAWING

As we begin the book, let us take note of the broad field of opportunity afforded the figure draftsman. Starting with the comic or simple line drawings of the newspaper, it extends all the way up through every kind of poster, display, and magazine advertising, through covers and story illustration to the realms of fine art, portraiture, sculpture, and mural decoration. Figure drawing presents the broadest opportunity from the standpoint of earning of any artistic endeavor. Coupled with this fact is the great advantage that all these uses are so interrelated that success in one almost assures success in another.

The interrelation of all these uses springs from the fact that all figure drawing is based on the same fundamentals which can be applied no matter what use the work is put to. This brings a further great advantage to the figure man in that he has a constant market if he is capable of good work. The market is constant because his work fits into so many notches in the cycle of buying and selling which must always be present barring financial collapse. To sell one must advertise, to advertise one must have advertising space, to have advertising space there must be attractively illustrated magazines, billboards, and other mediums. So starts the chain of uses of which the artist is an integral part.

To top it all, it becomes the most fascinating of any art effort because it offers such endless variety, encompassing so much that it ever remains new and stimulating. Dealing with the human aspects of life it runs the gamut of expression, emotion, gesture, environment, and the interpretation of character. What other fields of effort offer so great a variety for interest and genuine relief from monotony? I speak of this to build within you that confidence that all is well

once you arrive at your destination; your real concern is making the journey.

Art in its broadest sense is a language, a message that can be expressed better in no other way. It tells us what a product looks like and how we can use it. It describes the clothes and even the manners of other times. In a war poster it incites us to action; in a magazine it makes characters alive and vivid. It projects an idea visually, so that before a brick is laid we may see, before our eyes, the finished building.

There was a time when the artist withdrew to a bare attic to live in seclusion for an ideal. For subject, a plate of apples sufficed. Today, however, art has become an integral part of our lives, and the successful artist cannot set himself apart. He must do a certain job, in a definite manner, to a definite purpose, and with a specified date of delivery.

Start at once to take a new interest in people. Look for typical characters everywhere. Familiarize yourself with the characteristics and details that distinguish them. What is arrogance in terms of light and shadow, form and color? What lines give frustration and forlorn hope to people? What is the gesture in relation to the emotion? Why is a certain childish face adorable, a certain adult face suspicious and untrustworthy? You must search for the answers to these questions and be able to make them clear to your public. This knowledge will in time become a part of you, but it can come only from observation and understanding.

Try to develop the habit of observing your surroundings carefully. Some day you may want to place a figure in a similar atmosphere. You cannot succeed completely with the figure unless you can draw the details of the setting. So begin now to collect a file of the details that give a setting its "atmosphere."

Learn to observe significant details. You must be concerned with more than Martha's hairdress. Precisely why does Martha in a formal gown look so different in shorts or slacks? How do the folds of her dress break at the floor when she sits down?

Watch emotional gestures and expressions. What does a girl do with her hands when she says, "Oh, that's wonderful!"? Or with her feet when she drops into a chair and says, "Gosh, I'm tired!"? What does a mother's face register when she appeals to the doctor, "Is there no hope?" Or a child's when he says, "Gee, that's good!"? You must have more than mere technical ability to produce a good drawing.

Nearly every successful artist has a particular interest or drive or passion that gives direction to his technical skill. Often it is an absorption in some one phase of life. Harold von Schmidt, for example, loves the outdoors, rural life, horses, the pioneer, drama, and action. His work breathes the fire that is in him. Harry Anderson loves plain American people — the old family doctor, the little white cottage. Norman Rockwell, a great portrayer of character, loves a gnarled old hand that has done a lifetime of work, a shoe that has seen better days. His tender and sympathetic attitude toward humanity, implemented by his marvelous technical ability, has won him his place in the world of art. Jon Whitcomb and Al Parker are at the top because they can set down a poignant, up-to-the-minute portrayal of young America. The Clark brothers have a fondness for drawing the Old West and frontier days, and have been most successful at it. Maude Fangel loved babies and drew them beautifully. None of these people could have reached the pinnacle without their inner drives. Yet none could have arrived there without being able to draw well.

I do not strongly recommend becoming "helper" to a successful artist in order to gain background. More often than not, it is a discouraging experience. The reason is that you are continually matching your humble efforts against the stellar performance of your employer. You are not thinking and observing for yourself. You are usually dreaming, developing an inferiority complex, becoming an imitator. Remember: artists have no jealously guarded professional secrets. How often have I heard students say, "If I could just watch that man work, I'm sure I could get ahead!" Getting ahead does not happen that way. The only mystery, if such it may be called, is the personal interpretation of the individual artist. He himself probably does not know his own "secret." Fundamentals you must master, but you can never do so by watching another man paint. You have to reason them out for yourself.

Before you decide what type of drawing you want to concentrate on, it would be wise to consider your particular background of experience. If you have been brought up on a farm, for instance, you are much more likely to succeed in interpreting life on a farm than in depicting Long Island society life. Don't ignore the intimate knowledge you have gained from long, everyday acquaintance. All of us tend to discount our own experience and knowledge—to consider *our* background dull and commonplace. But that is a serious mistake. No background is barren of artistic material. The artist who grew up in poverty can create just as much beauty in drawing tumble-down sheds as another artist might in drawing ornate and luxurious settings. As a matter of fact, he is apt to know much more about life, and his art is likely to have a broader appeal. Today great interest has developed in the "American Scene." Simple homeliness is its general keynote. Our advertising and much of our illustration, however, demand the sophisticated and the smart, but it is wise to bear in mind this newer trend, for which a humble background is no handicap.

It is true that most artists must be prepared to handle any sort of subject on demand. But gradually each one will be chosen for the thing he does best. If you do not want to be typed or "catalogued," you will have to work hard to widen your scope. It means learning broad drawing principles (everything has proportion, three dimensions, texture, color, light, and shadow) so that you will not be floored by commissions that may call for a bit of still life, a landscape, an animal, a particular texture such as satin or knitted wool. If you learn to observe, the demands should not tax your technical capacity, because the rendering of all form is based upon the way light falls upon it and the way light affects its value and color. Furthermore, you can always do research on any unfamiliar subject. Most artists spend as much time in obtaining suitable data as in actual drawing or painting.

The fundamentals of painting and drawing are the same. Perhaps it might be said that drawing in general does not attempt to render the subtleties of values, edges, and planes or modeling that may be obtained in paint. In any medium, however, the artist is confronted with the same problems: he will have to consider the horizon and viewpoint; he will have to set down properly length, breadth, and thickness (in so far as he is able on the flat surface); he will have to consider, in short, the elements that I am talking about in this book.

The nude human figure must serve as the basis for all figure study. It is impossible to draw the clothed or draped figure without a knowledge of the structure and form of the figure underneath. The artist who cannot put the figure together properly does not have one chance in a thousand of success—either as a figure draftsman or as a painter. It would be as reasonable to expect to become a surgeon without studying anatomy. If you are offended by the sight of the body the Almighty gave us to live in, then put this book aside at once and likewise give up all thought of a career in art. Since all of us are either male or female, and since the figures of the two sexes differ so radically in construction and appearance (a woman in slacks is *not* a man in pants, even when she has a short haircut), it is fantastic to conceive of a study of figure drawing that did not analyze the many differences. I have been engaged in almost every type of commercial art, and my experience confirms the fact that the study of the nude is indispensable to any art career that requires figure drawing. A vocational course without such study is a deplorable waste of time. Life classes generally work from the living model; hence I have tried to supply drawings that will serve as a substitute.

Broadly speaking, there are two kinds of drawing: linear and solid. Linear drawing—for example, a floor plan—embraces design or scale. Solid drawing attempts to render bulk or three-dimensional quality on a flat plane of paper or canvas. The first involves no consideration of light and shadow. The latter gives it every consideration. It is possible, however, without light and shadow, to make a flat or outline drawing of a figure and still suggest its bulk. Therefore it is logical to begin with the figure in flat dimension—start out with proportion, carry it from the flat to the round, and then proceed to render the bulk in space or in terms of light and shadow.

The eye perceives form much more readily by contour or edge than by the modeling. Yet there is really no outline on form; rather, there is a silhouette of contour, encompassing as much of the form as we can see from a single viewpoint. We must of necessity limit that form some way. So we draw a line—an outline. An outline truly belongs within the category of flat rendering, though it can be accompanied by the use of light and shadow. The painter dispenses with outline because he can define contours against other masses or build out the form in relief by the use of values.

You must understand the difference between contour and line. A piece of wire presents a line. A contour is an edge. That edge may be a sharp limitation to the form (the edges of a cube) or a rounded and disappearing limitation (the contour of a sphere). Many contours pass in front of one another, like the contours of an undulating landscape. Line figure drawing, even as landscape drawing, demands foreshortening in order to produce the effect of solid form. You cannot outline a figure with a bent wire and hope to render its solid aspect. Look for two kinds of lines: the flowing or rhythmic line, weaving it about the form; and, for the sake of stability and structure, the contrasting straight or angular line.

Line can have infinite variety, or it can be intensely monotonous. Even if you start with a bent wire, you need not make it entirely monotonous. You can vary the weight of line. When you are drawing a contour that is near a very light area, you can use a light line or even omit it entirely. When the line represents a contour that is dark and strong, you can give it more weight and vitality. The slightest outline drawing can be inventive and expressive.

Take up your pencil and begin to swing it over your paper; then let it down. That is a "free" line, a "rhythmic" line. Now, grasping your pencil lightly between thumb and index finger, draw lightly or delicately. Then bear down as though you really meant it. That is a "variable" line. See if you can draw a straight line and then set down another parallel to it. That is a "studied" line.

If you have considered a line as merely a mark, it may be a revelation to you that line alone possesses so much variation that you can worry over it for the rest of your days. Remember that line is something to turn to when your drawings are dull. You can start expressing your individuality with the kinds of line you draw.

Now to the figure. What is the height-to-width relationship of an ideal figure? An ideal figure standing straight must fit within a certain rectangle. What is that rectangle? See drawing, page 26. The simplest and most convenient unit for measuring the figure is the head. A normal person will fall short of our ideal by half a head— he will measure only seven and a half heads instead of eight. You need not take eight heads as an absolute measure. Your ideal man may have any proportions you wish, but he is usually made tall. On pages 26 to 29 you will find various proportions in head units. Note that at any time you can vary your proportions to suit the particular problem. Study these carefully and draw them, two or three times, for you will use them, consciously or not, every time you set up a figure. Some artists prefer the legs even a little longer than shown. But, if the foot is shown tipped down in perspective, it will add considerable length and be about right.

It is remarkable that most beginners' work looks alike. Analyzing it, I have found certain characteristics that should be mentioned here. I suggest that you compare this list with your own work to see if you can locate some of the characteristics for improvement.

1. *Consistently gray throughout.*

   What to do: First get a soft pencil that will make a good black.

   Pick out the blacks in your subject and state them strongly.

   By contrast, leave areas of white where subject is white or very light.

   Avoid putting overstated grays in light areas.

   Do not surround things that are light with heavy lines.

2. An overabundance of small fuzzy line.

Do not "pet" in your line, draw it cleanly with long sweep.

Do not shade with a multitude of little "pecky" strokes.

Use the side of the lead with the pencil laid almost flat for your modeling and shadows.

3. Features misplaced in a head.

Learn what the construction lines of the head are and how spaced. (See Head Drawing.)

Build the features into the correct spaces.

4. Rubbed and dirty, usually in a roll.

Spray with fixative. If on thin paper, mount on heavier stock.

Try never to break the surface of your paper. This is very bad. If you have done so, start over. Keep your drawings flat. Keep untouched areas scrupulously clean with a kneaded eraser.

5. Too many mediums in same picture.

Make your subject in one medium. Do not combine wax crayons with pencil, or pastel with something else. Make it all pencil, all crayon, all pastel, all water color, or all pen and ink. It gives a certain consistency. Later on you may combine different mediums effectively but do not start that way.

6. The tendency to use tinted papers.

A black and white drawing looks better on white paper than anything else.

If you have to use tinted paper, then work in a color that is harmonious. For instance a brown or red conte crayon on a tan or cream paper.

It is better to put your color on white for clarity.

7. Copies of movie stars.

This gets intensely monotonous to anyone inspecting a beginner's work. The heads are usually badly lighted from a drawing standpoint. Take a head that is not well known.

8. Bad arrangement.

If you are doing a vignetted head, plan interesting and attractive shapes. Don't run over to the edge of the paper unless whole space is to be squared off.

9. Highlights in chalk.

It takes a very skillful artist to do this successfully.

10. Uninteresting subjects.

Just a costume does not make a picture. Every picture should have some interest if possible other than a technical demonstration. Heads should portray character, or expression. Other subjects should have mood or action or sentiment to make it interesting.

Water color is perhaps the most tricky medium of all. Yet most beginners take to it. Water color to be effective should be broad in treatment, with large loose washes, and not too finicky. If you find yourself stippling and pecking you can be pretty sure it will not be liked.

Water color should have a feeling of the "accidental" or color that has done something of its own and dried that way. Lovely effects are obtained by dampening an area first and then flowing the color into the wet area. Use a real water color paper or board, for it can get very messy on a soft and very absorbent paper. The less you have to go over what you have once put down, the better. Generally water-colorists prefer not to leave a lot of pencil, especially dark or shaded pencil showing through. Some water-colorists work by washing in a general tone, scrubbing out the lights with a soft sponge or brush, and washing in the halftones and darks over the original tone. If you are unable to handle water color in any other way than by pecking in little strokes, I would suggest you try pastel which can be spread and rubbed at will. Oil paint has the advantage that it stays wet long enough to maneuver the color as you wish.

IDEAL PROPORTION, MALE

HEAD UNITS

8

Chin
7

⅓ Shoulders

Nipples
6

Navel
5

⅓ Hips

Crotch
4

⅓ Buttocks

Fingers
3

Bottom of Knees
2

1

Heels

1 Head

I — Head

Calves drop back of Buttocks and Shoulders

FEET ‹Male Figure is 2 ⅓ heads wide›

6 FT

9 inches

Shoulders at 5'-0"
5 FT

4 FT

3 FT

2 FT

1 FT

Lower legs are back of middle line thru figure

Ideal height of girl in heads

Take any desired height, or place points for top of head and heels. Divide into eighths. Two and one third of these units will be the relative width for the male figure. It is not necessary at this stage to attempt to render the anatomy correctly. But fix in your mind the divisions.

Draw the figure in the three positions: front, side, and back. Note the comparative widths at shoulders, hips, and calves. Note that the space between nipples is one head unit. The waist is a little wider than one head unit. The wrist drops just below the crotch. The elbows are about on a line with the navel. The knees are just above the lower quarter of the figure. The shoulders are one-sixth of the way down. The proportions are also given in feet so that you may accurately relate your figure to furniture and interiors.

IDEAL PROPORTION, FEMALE

HEAD UNITS

IDEAL MALE HEIGHT 6 FT
FEET
Height with heels
Actual height
5'-8"

Female figure is 2 heads wide

8

8½ inches

Chin
7
⅓rd = Shoulders

5 FT

TWO HEADS

TWO HEADS

6 ⅙th Nipples
-⅓rd Breasts

4 FT

Elbows-Waist
5 ⅙th Navel

ONE HEAD

ONE HEAD

Middle Point
4
⅓rd Crotch

3 FT

1½ Heads

3

TABLE HEIGHT
2'-4"

2 FT

Bottom of Knees
2

Height of a chair
1'-6"

ONE HEAD

1 FT

1

Heels
Shoe Heels

The female figure is relatively narrower—two heads at the widest point. The nipples are slightly lower than in the male. The waistline measures one head unit across. In front the thighs are slightly wider than the armpits, narrower in back. It is optional whether or not you draw the legs even a little longer from the knees down. Wrists are even with crotch. Five feet eight inches (in heels) is considered an ideal height for a girl. Actually, of course, the average girl has shorter legs and somewhat heavier thighs. Note carefully that the female navel is below the waistline; the male, above or even with it. The nipples and navel are one head apart, but both are dropped below the head divisions. The elbow is above the navel. It is important that you learn the variations between the male and female figure.

VARIOUS STANDARDS OF PROPORTION

NORMAL, 7½ HDS

THE ACADEMIC PROPORTIONS USED IN MOST SCHOOLS. (RATHER DUMPY)

2 HEADS

MIDDLE

IDEALISTIC, 8 HDS

MOST ARTISTS ACCEPT 8 HEADS AS NORMAL

2 ⅓ HEADS

MIDDLE

FASHION, 8 ½ HDS

ACCEPTED

2 ⅓ or ½ HEADS

MIDDLE

HEROIC. 9 HDS

2 ⅔ HEADS

Sculpture

MIDDLE

You can see at a glance why the actual or normal proportions are not very satisfactory. All academic drawings based on normal proportions have this dumpy, old-fashioned look. Most fashion artists stretch the figure even beyond eight heads, and in allegorical or heroic figures the "superhuman" type — nine heads — may be used effectively. Note at what point, or head unit, the middle of the figure falls in each. It would be well to draw the side and back in these various proportions, using the previous page for a general guide but changing the proportion. You can control the appearance of height or shortness in any figure by the relative size of the head you use.

28

ADULT

ADULT HEADS

15 Yrs

9 inches

7½

9 inches

9"   9"   7½"   7"   6½"   6"

ADULT   15 YRS   10 YRS   5 YRS   3 YRS   1 YR

The growth of the head is very gradual, only adding 3 inches up and down from the first year to adulthood. The legs grow nearly twice as fast as the torso.

10 YRS = 7 HDS @ 7½"

5 YRS = 6 HDS @ 7"

3 YRS = 5 HDS @ 6½"

1 YR = 4 HDS @ 6"

These proportions have been worked out with a great deal of effort and, as far as I know, have never before been put down for the artist. The scale assumes that the child will grow to be an ideal adult of eight head units. If, for instance, you want to draw a man or a woman (about half a head shorter than you would draw the man)

with a five-year-old boy, you have here his relative height. Children under ten are made a little shorter and chubbier than normal, since this effect is considered more desirable; those over ten, a little taller than normal — for the same reason.

THE FLAT DIAGRAM

Vanishing point.

HOW TO PROJECT THE "FLAT DIAGRAM" ONTO THE GROUND PLANE

This will prove most useful when you have to draw without a model and in foreshortening

You will learn later how to build the solid from the flat diagram.

Chin
7
NIPPLE
6
NAVEL
5
CROTCH
4
2 1/3 hds
3
Bottom OF KNEE
2
1
HEEL
A · B · C
FLAT DIAGRAM

Fill in the 16 units by following the Flat Diagram

Using two planes

Shadows can be drawn by this plan. It is a "guide" for the solid in perspective.

THE FLAT DIAGRAM IS NO MORE THAN A TRACING OF A SHADOW - WITH ONLY TWO DIMENSIONS - BUT IT IS OUR "MAP". WE CAN'T DO WITHOUT IT - UNTIL WE KNOW THE WAY.

Draw Diagonals A thru D to E. Line. E H established. Then F to G and so on until there are 8 spaces.

To V.P.
To Vanishing point
To V.P.

Divide by diagonals until there are 8 cross spaces.

1st Division
1st
2d Division
3rd Diag.
2d diagonal
OPTIONAL DEPTH FOR RECTANGLE

3rd diagonal
2d diagonal
1st diagonal
OPTIONAL DEPTH.

Flat Diagram Sitting pose 3 Planes

Two ways of rendering the "Box" of the Flat Diagram in perspective. You are urged to learn this now. It will help you out of many difficulties later on.

Showing how the principle applies to difficult foreshortening to be explained.

THE FLAT DIAGRAM
OTHER IMPORTANT USES OF THE "MAP" OR FLAT DIAGRAM.

← To Vanishing Point

LEFT EAR
RIGHT EAR
CHIN
LEFT SHOULDER
RT SHOULDER
LFT. NIPPLE
RT NIPPLE
LFT. ELBOW
Navel
RT. ELBOW
LFT HIP
RT HIP
CROTCH

HORIZON

HAND

You will build the three dimensional figure later

RT KNEE
LFT KNEE

To V.Pt.

RT ANKLE
LFT ANKLE
FEET

$\frac{1}{3}$ head $\frac{1}{3}$

Shoulders

Nipples

Navel

CROTCH

Bottom of Knees
$\frac{1}{2}$

Heels

All points of the figure can be put in perspective with the "Map" as guide

Quick "Set up" in perspective

Quick "Set up" of the "Map".

Try drawing the "Map" in perspective

HORIZON

The proportions of one figure can easily be projected by perspective to others.

QUICK SET-UP OF PROPORTIONS

3/4

Shoulders 1/3

Waist 2/3

1/2 CROTCH

1/4

1hd

2 hds

3 hds

A

Knees

1/2

1
2
3
4

1hd — head

Shoulders 1/3

2hds NIPPLES

3hds NAVEL 2/3

HIPS.

4hds 1/2 CROTCH

KNEES

1/2

A simple method of finding lengths of extended limbs. Later you will do this in perspective.

PROPORTION IN RELATION TO THE HORIZON

How to build your picture and figures from any eye level (or Horizon, which means the same)

1	2	3	4	5	6
EYE LEVEL SELECTED	(HORIZON)				
Select a placement for the Horizon	Establish height of first figure. (Any height)	Set point for feet of 2ᵈ Figure. (Place anywhere)	Draw line through point to Horizon	Then back to "A" at top 1st Figure	Erect perpendicular at "C". CB is 2ᵈ Figure

7	8	9	10	11	12
Divide into 4ths.	Build figures. If you want more—	Take another point "D" thru "C" to Horizon	Divide as you did before	Complete 3rd Fig.	Build your picture to same Horizon.

Rule: Horizon must cross all similar figures on a level plane at the same point. (above, at knees)

HOW TO LAY OUT THUMBNAIL SKETCHES FOR FIGURE PLACEMENTS AND SIZES

From one figure you can get any number

HORIZON MAY BE PLACED ABOVE FIGURES
HORIZON

Take a little off for a woman's figure

A figure may run out of picture

One figure is WRONG. Explain why.

For close figure find half of it.

Here are two levels

John and Mary, how they look if we are sitting near them on the sand.

The picture changes if we stand. The horizon goes up with us.

Now if we lie down the horizon drops too. The perspective changes.

We walk backward and upward on the beach. Horizon rises above, now.

If we get beneath them so does the horizon. The figures change again.

Now the Horizon moves up beyond the picture. But it still affects figures—

Even when we see them from nearly directly overhead. No matter

(From 3 stories, or 10 stories up, it will put them the same distance below the HORIZON.)

where we are, every figure is affected by our own eye level, or "MY Horizon"

SOME THINGS THAT MAY HAPPEN WHEN FIGURES ARE NOT RELATED TO A SINGLE TRUE HORIZON

The figures appear tipped

or somehow wrong—

John may be falling—or

Mary doing gymnastics

Mary gets too big—or she

may get too small—or

appear to be diving—

YOUR DRAWING IS REJECTED AND NO ONE REALLY SEEMS TO KNOW WHAT IS WRONG

Thus endeth John and Mary

35

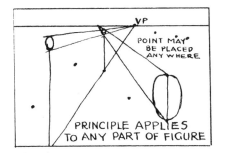

Many artists have difficulty in placing figures in their picture and properly relating them to each other, especially if the complete figure is not shown. The solution is to draw a key figure for standing or sitting poses. Either the whole figure or any part of it can then be scaled with the horizon. *AB* is taken as the head measurement and applied to all standing figures; *CD* to the sitting figures. This applies *when all figures are on the same ground plane.* (On page 37 there is an explanation of how to proceed when the figures are at different levels.) You can place a point anywhere within your space and find the relative size of the figure or portion of the figure at precisely that spot. Obviously everything else should be drawn to the same horizon and scaled so that the figures are relative. For instance, draw a key horse or cow or chair or boat. The important thing is that all figures retain their size relationships, no matter how close or distant. A picture can have only one horizon, and only one station point. The horizon moves up or down with the observer. It is not possible to look over the horizon, for it is constituted by the eye level or lens level of the subject. The horizon on an open, flat plane of land or water is visible. Among hills or indoors it may not be actually visible, but your eye level determines it. If you do not understand perspective, there is a good book on the subject, *Perspective Made Easy,* available at most booksellers.

You can "hang" your figures on the Horizon line by making it cut through similar figures in the same place. This keeps them on the same ground plane. Note Horizon cuts men at waist and the seated women at chin. The one standing woman at left is drawn relative to the men. Simple?

You can also "hang" heads on the Horizon line. In this case it cuts men's heads at the mouth, the womens at the eyes.

Here we have measured a proportionate distance down from the Horizon. I have taken two heads as an optional space.

WE BEGIN TO DRAW: FIRST THE MANNIKIN FRAME

THE FIRST PROBLEM: HOW SHALL THE WEIGHT BE CARRIED?

HEAD
Shoulder
NIPPLES
NAVEL
CROTCH
BOTTOM OF KNEES

PROPORTION LINE   MANNIKIN FRAME   SIDE   WEIGHT ON RT. FOOT   WT. ON LFT. FOOT   WT. ON BOTH FEET

WEIGHT ON PELVIS   WT. ONE KNEE, ONE FOOT   BOTH KNEES   HANDS AND KNEES   ONE FOOT ONLY

ALL FIGURE ACTION SHOULD
BE BASED ON A DISTRIBUTION
OF THE WEIGHT OF THE BODY

ON ALL FOURS   COMBINATION HANDS, PELVIS AND FEET   SUSPENDED   BACK AND PELVIS

38

MOVEMENT IN THE MANNIKIN FRAME

LET US STRIVE FOR LIFE AND ACTION FROM THE VERY BEGINNING. DRAW, DRAW.

THESE ARE "STATIONARY PIVOTS"

TRY TO "FEEL A CENTER OF GRAVITY." DISTRIBUTE THE WEIGHT OVER A CENTRAL POINT. MAKE NUMEROUS STUDIES.

THESE ARE "MOVING PIVOTS"

THE MAIN LINE OF BALANCE SHOULD LEAN IN THE DIRECTION OF THE MOVEMENT. TRY SOME NOW.

YOUR FIGURES MAY BE BUILT UPON CURVED LINES FOR MOVEMENT AND GRACE. AVOID RIGHT ANGLES

HEAD.
SHOULDERS

NIPPLE

NAVEL

CROTCH

BOTTOM OF KNEES

HEELS

PROPORTION LINE   FRONT   BACK   3/4 BACK   SIDE   3/4 FRONT

ALL THE TIME YOU SPEND ON THIS FELLOW PAYS BIG DIVIDENDS. LEARN ALL ABOUT HIM.

DRAW A "CAPE" LIKE THIS

CURVE

CURVE THE LEGS

PUSH BACK →

NEVER DRAW THE LIMBS STRAIGHT AND STIFF AND WITHOUT "SPRING"

TWO DISCS FOR NOW

LAY THE "CAPE" OVER BALL OF CHEST 2 HDS

3 HDS.

THIS IS A SIMPLIFIED VERSION OF THE ACTUAL FRAME - ALL YOU NEED FOR A START

EXPERIMENTING WITH THE MANNIKIN FRAME

DO A LOT OF EXPERIMENTING. REMEMBER THAT MOST OF THE ACTION IN YOUR FIGURES MUST COME FROM YOU "AS YOU FEEL IT" RATHER THAN FROM A MODEL.

YOU WILL SOON LEARN TO EXPRESS YOURSELF. A VITAL EXPRESSION IS MORE IMPORTANT HERE THAN ACCURACY.

YOU CAN USE THIS TYPE OF SKELETON WHEN PLANNING ROUGHS, LAYOUTS, COMPOSITIONS.

OUTLINES IN RELATION TO SOLID FORM

A. LET US ASSUME WE HAVE OUTLINES OF THREE CIRCLES SET ON 3 ADJACENT PLANES.

ALL SOLIDS MUST HAVE THESE THREE DIMENSIONS.

1 LENGTH

2 BREADTH

3 THICKNESS

B. BY MOVING CIRCLES FORWARD TO A COMMON CENTER, WE PRODUCE A "SOLID" BALL.

NOW TAKE A COMMON OBJECT.

THE "OUTLINES" OF EACH PLANE MAY BE VERY DIFFERENT, BUT PUT TOGETHER, FORM THE SOLID.

SO, IN DRAWING WE MUST ALWAYS TRY TO "FEEL" THE MIDDLE CONTOURS AS WELL AS THE EDGES. THE OUTLINES ALONE CAN SUGGEST SOLIDITY. WATCH HOW EDGES PASS ONE ANOTHER.

FLAT

SOLID

THIS WILL NOT BE EASY UNTIL YOU BECOME ABLE TO "THINK ALL AROUND" THE THING YOU HAPPEN TO BE DRAWING, TRULY KNOWING ALL OF THE FORM.

THE MANNIKIN FIGURE

The foregoing has given us a general framework to which we can now add a simplification of the bulk or solid aspect of the figure. It would be both tedious and superfluous if, every time we drew a figure, we went through the whole procedure of figure drawing. The artist will want to make roughs and sketches that can serve as an understructure for pose or action—perhaps to cover with clothing, perhaps to work out a pose that he will finish with a model. We must have some direct and quick way of indicating or setting up an experimental figure — one with which we can tell a story. The figure set up as suggested in the following pages will usually suffice. Properly done, it can always be developed into the more finished drawing. When you are drawing a mannikin figure, you need not be greatly concerned with the actual muscles or how they affect the surface. The mannikin in drawing is used much as is a "lay" figure, to indicate joints and the general proportion of framework and masses.

The mannikin serves a double purpose here. I believe that the student will do much better to set up the figure this way and get the "feel" of its parts in action than to begin at once with the live model. It will not only serve for rough sketches but will also become an ideal approach to the actual drawing of the figure from life or copy. If you have the frame and masses to begin with, you can later break them down into actual bone and muscle. Then you can more easily grasp the placing and functions of the muscles and what they do to the surface. I am of the opinion that to teach anatomy before proportion—before bulk and mass and action—is to put the cart before the horse. You cannot draw a muscle correctly without a fair estimate of the area it occupies within the figure, without an understanding of why it is there and of how it works.

Think of the figure in a plastic sense, or as something with three dimensions. It has weight that must be held up by a framework which is extremely mobile. The fleshy masses or bulk follows the frame. Some of these masses are knit together quite closely and adhere to the bony structure, whereas other masses are full and thick and will be affected in appearance by action.

If you have never studied anatomy, you may not know that the muscles fall naturally into groups or chunks attached in certain ways to the frame. We will not treat their physiological detail here, but consider them merely as parts interlocked or wedged together. Hence the human figure looks very much like our mannikin. The thorax, or chest, is egg-shaped and, as far as we are concerned, hollow. Over it is draped a cape of muscle extending across the chest and down the back to the base of the spine. Over the cape, in front, lie the shoulder muscles. The buttocks start halfway around in back, from the hips, and slant downward, ending in rather square creases. A V is formed by the slant above the middle crease. There is actually a V-shaped bone here, wedged between the two pelvic bones that support the spine. The chest is joined to the hips by two masses on either side. In back the calf wedges into the thigh, and in front there is the bulge of the knee.

Learn to draw this mannikin as well as you can. You will use it much more often than a careful anatomical rendering. Since it is in proportion in bulk and frame, it may also be treated in perspective. No artist could possibly afford a model for all his rough preliminary work—for layouts and ideas. Yet he cannot intelligently approach his final work without a preliminary draft. If only art directors would base their layouts on such mannikin figures, the finished figures would all stand on the same floor, and heads would not run off the page when drawn correctly.

ADDING BULK TO THE FRAME

THE GROUPS OF MUSCLES SIMPLIFIED.

DEVELOPING THE PREVIOUS FRAME WITH SIMPLIFIED MUSCLE GROUPS LAID ON TOP.

A SIMPLER MANNIKIN IF THE OTHER IS TOO DIFFICULT.

WE WILL STUDY THE "ACTUAL" BONE AND MUSCLE CONSTRUCTION LATER. GET THIS.

HERE IS A GROUP OF CYLINDERS. NOTE HOW THE ELLIPSES NARROW DOWN AS THEY NEAR THE EYE LEVEL, EITHER FROM ABOVE OR BELOW.

EYE LEVEL AND HORIZON

FROM THIS YOU GET THE PRINCIPLE OF PERSPECTIVE IN THE ROUND FORMS ON THE FIGURE.

TRY DRAWING YOUR MANNIKIN FIGURE TO THE HORIZON

VP

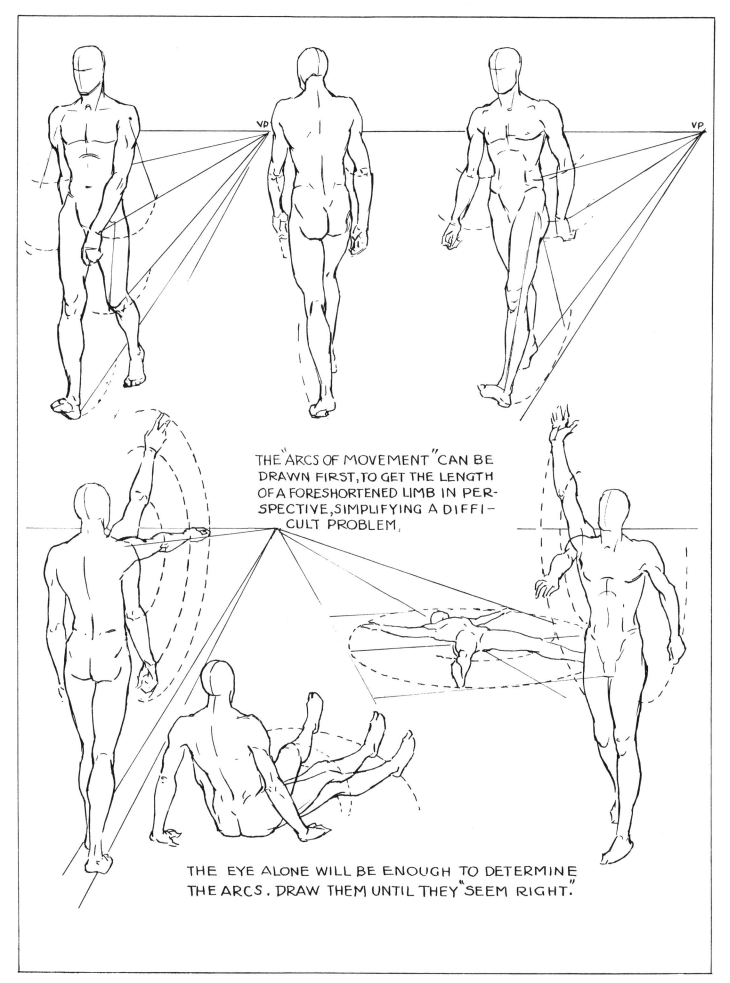

THE "ARCS OF MOVEMENT" CAN BE DRAWN FIRST, TO GET THE LENGTH OF A FORESHORTENED LIMB IN PERSPECTIVE, SIMPLIFYING A DIFFICULT PROBLEM.

THE EYE ALONE WILL BE ENOUGH TO DETERMINE THE ARCS. DRAW THEM UNTIL THEY "SEEM RIGHT."

IF YOU DO NOT UNDERSTAND PERSPECTIVE, IT IS ADVISED TO GET A GOOD BOOK ON THE SUBJECT. YOU MUST KNOW IT EVENTUALLY TO SUCCEED. YOU CANNOT SET UP A GOOD DRAWING WITHOUT IT.

V.P SELECTED EYE LEVEL (HORIZON)

HORIZON.

VP.

(Parallel Perspective) on this FIGURE.

FROM THIS MAN

FEET RAISED TO HERE

Measuring Line

(FEET)

To Vanishing Point.

FIGURE ONE.
(ALL SCALED FROM HIM)

EVERY FIGURE IS RELATED IN SIZE TO EVERY OTHER FIGURE AND ALL MUST BE DRAWN IN PERSPECTIVE TO THE SAME EYE LEVEL OR HORIZON.

47

DRAW THE "BOX" IN ROUGH PERSPECTIVE. DIVIDE BY DIAGONALS. BUILD MANNIKIN.

SKETCH YOUR "RINGS" IN THE 4 SECTIONS OF THE BOX.

THINK IN TERMS OF THE SOLID.

LANDMARKS YOU SHOULD KNOW

SURFACE CHARACTERISTICS THAT GIVE "PUNCH" TO THE FIGURE DRAWN WITHOUT A MODEL

BONE

BONE NEAR SURFACE

CONVEX LINE

LINE BENDS IN HERE, TOP LINE PASSES UNDER

BONE
PATELLA
BONE

OUTLINE PASSES

CALF HIGH ON THE OUTSIDE, LOW INSIDE

OUTLINE BENDS IN

SHIN BONE

ANKLE HIGH INSIDE, LOW OUTSIDE

LINE PASSES

BALL OF BIG TOE

INSIDE

FURROWS

LINE PASSES HIGH

LINE PASSES LOW

CALF "WEDGES" INTO UPPER LEG IN BACK

HIGH

LOW

LINE PASSES

SHOW THIS TENDON

CORDS AT PIT OF NECK
5 HOLLOWS
DELTOID DIPS IN SLIGHTLY
1 2 3 4 5

LINES PASS

THESE ARE MUSCLES INTERLACING WITH RIBS

FURROW

LINE PASSES

CORD AND HOLLOWS
BONE
NAVEL, NIPPLE, BONE IN SHOULDER FALL IN STRAIGHT LINE.
CONVEX LINE TO THE OUTSIDE
FURROW

FURROW

LINE PASSES

DIP

LINES PASS

CONVEX

THE ELBOW IS NEVER STRAIGHT AND STIFF LIKE A MITERED CORNER

CONVEX

DIP
BONE
DIP
BONE

STUDY THESE "LANDMARKS" CAREFULLY.
THEY WILL KEEP YOUR FIGURES FROM
LOOKING FLABBY AND SHAPELESS.
LATER, WHEN YOU TAKE UP THE ACTUAL
BONE AND MUSCLE, YOU WILL HAVE THE
IMPORTANT THINGS TO LOOK FOR.

LANDMARKS YOU SHOULD KNOW

SURFACE CHARACTERISTICS ON THE BACK OF THE MALE FIGURE. TO MEMORIZE.

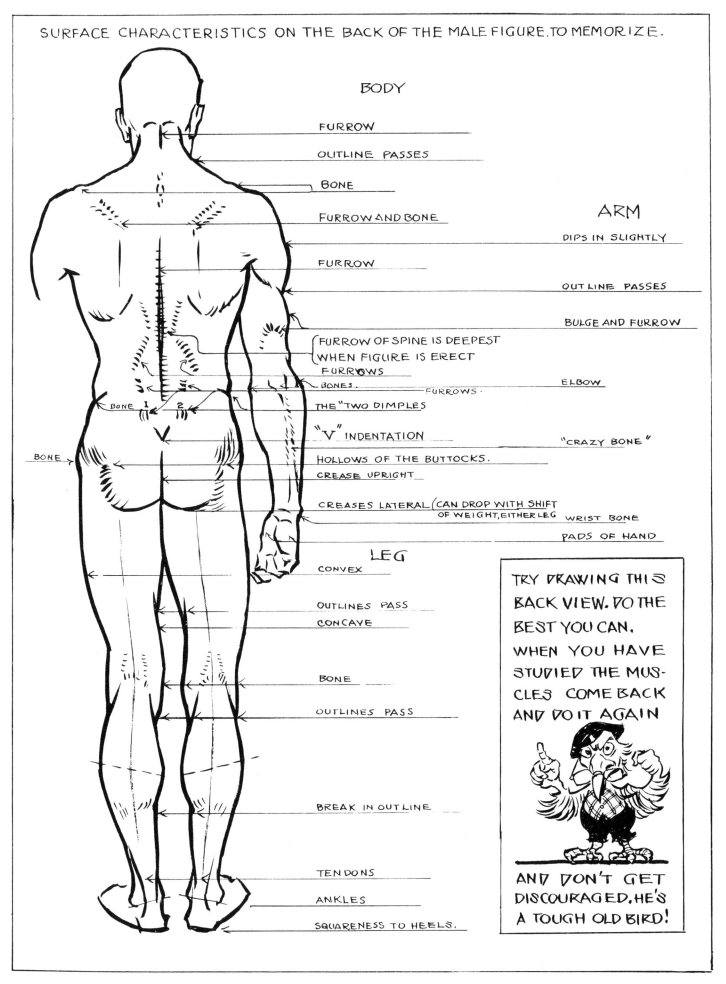

BODY

FURROW

OUTLINE PASSES

BONE

FURROW AND BONE

FURROW

FURROW OF SPINE IS DEEPEST
WHEN FIGURE IS ERECT

FURROWS

BONES.

BONE 1 2

FURROWS.

THE "TWO DIMPLES

"V" INDENTATION

HOLLOWS OF THE BUTTOCKS.

CREASE UPRIGHT

CREASES LATERAL (CAN DROP WITH SHIFT
OF WEIGHT, EITHER LEG

BONE

ARM

DIPS IN SLIGHTLY

OUTLINE PASSES

BULGE AND FURROW

ELBOW

"CRAZY BONE"

WRIST BONE

PADS OF HAND

LEG

CONVEX

OUTLINES PASS

CONCAVE

BONE

OUTLINES PASS

BREAK IN OUTLINE

TENDONS

ANKLES

SQUARENESS TO HEELS.

TRY DRAWING THIS
BACK VIEW. DO THE
BEST YOU CAN.
WHEN YOU HAVE
STUDIED THE MUS-
CLES COME BACK
AND DO IT AGAIN

AND DON'T GET
DISCOURAGED. HE'S
A TOUGH OLD BIRD!

LEARNING TO "FEEL" AND SET UP THE FIGURE IN ACTION IS NOT AS DIFFICULT AS IT LOOKS

DRAW SOME OF THESE BUT DRAW MANY OF YOUR OWN

KEEP YOUR DRAWINGS FREE AND SKETCHY. DRAW MANY FIGURES AT VARIOUS EYE LEVELS.

THE FEMALE MANNIKIN

THE MAIN DIFFERENCE BETWEEN THE MALE AND FEMALE MANNIKIN IS IN THE PELVIS (DISCS). THE HIP BONES COME UP TO THE LINE OF THE NAVEL (MALE, THEY ARE TWO OR THREE INCHES BELOW). THE FEMALE WAISTLINE IS ABOVE THE NAVEL, THE MALE AT OR JUST BELOW. FEMALE RIB CASE IS SMALLER, PELVIS WIDER AND DEEPER, SHOULDERS NARROWER. "CAPE" DROPS IN FRONT TO INCLUDE BREASTS.

A SIMPLE WAY OF GETTING FEMALE PROPORTIONS-TAKE ⅓ TO KNEES- ⅔ TO WAIST, 3/3 TO TOP OF HEAD.

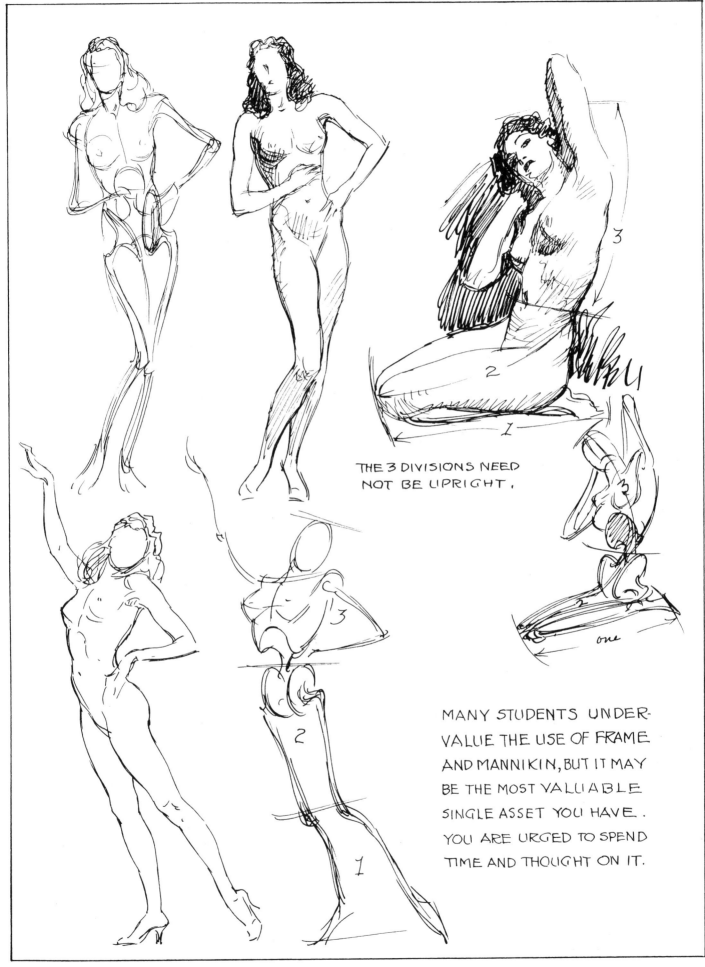

THE 3 DIVISIONS NEED
NOT BE UPRIGHT.

MANY STUDENTS UNDER-
VALUE THE USE OF FRAME
AND MANNIKIN, BUT IT MAY
BE THE MOST VALUABLE
SINGLE ASSET YOU HAVE.
YOU ARE URGED TO SPEND
TIME AND THOUGHT ON IT.

THE MALE AND FEMALE SKELETONS

HEADS
8

"IDEAL" PROPORTIONS USED

HEADS
8

CLAVICLE

SCAPULA

STERNUM

HUMERUS

SPINE

PELVIS

SACRUM

RADIUS

ULNA

GT. TROCHANTER

PUBIS

FEMUR

PATELLA

TIBIA

FIBULA

NAVEL

■ INDICATES WHERE
BONE SHOWS ON SURFACE

✱ NOTE DIFFERENCE IN
SHAPE OF FEMALE PELVIS

56

II. THE BONES AND MUSCLES

The further you go in the study of anatomy, the more interesting it becomes. Made of soft and pliable material, elastic yet strong, capable of unlimited movement and of performing countless tasks, operating on self-generated power, and repairing or renewing itself over a period of time in which the strongest of steel parts would wear out—the human body is indeed an engineering miracle.

On the opposite page the male and female skeletons have been set up. I have kept the head units alongside so that you may relate the bones to the figure in correct proportion.

The skeleton, though strong, is really not so rigid as it appears. Though the spine has a rigid base in the pelvis, it possesses great flexibility; and the ribs, too, though they are fastened firmly into the spine, are flexible. All the bones are held together and upright by cartilage and muscle, and the joints operate on a ball-and-socket plan with a "stop" for stability. The whole structure collapses with a loss of consciousness.

Strain upon the muscles can usually be transferred to the bony structure. The weight of a heavy load, for example, is largely taken over by the bones, leaving the muscles free to propel the limbs. Bones also form a protection to delicate organs and parts. The skull protects the eyes, the brain, and the delicate inner parts of the throat. The ribs and pelvis protect the heart, lungs, and other organs. Where protection is most needed, the bone comes closest to the surface.

It is very important for the artist to know that no bone is perfectly straight. An arm or a leg drawn with a perfectly straight bone will be rigid and stiff-looking. Curvature in the bones has much to do with the rhythm and action of a figure. It helps make it appear alive.

The chief differences between the male and female skeletons are the proportionately larger pelvis in the female and the proportionately larger thorax, or rib case, in the male. These differences account for the wider shoulders and narrower hips of the male; the longer waistline, lower buttocks, and wider hips of the female. They also cause the female arms to flare out wider when they are swinging back and forth and the femur, or thigh bone, to be a little more oblique. The hair and breasts, of course, distinguish the female figure, but they are merely its most obvious characteristics. The female is different from head to toe. The jaw is less developed. The neck is more slender. The hands are smaller and much more delicate. The muscles of the arms are smaller and much less in evidence. The waistline is higher. The great trochanter of the femur extends out farther; the buttocks are fuller, rounder, and lower. The thighs are flatter and wider. The calf is much less developed. The ankles and wrists are smaller. The feet are smaller and more arched. The muscles, in general, are less prominent, more straplike—all but those of the thighs and buttocks, which are proportionately larger and stronger in the female. This extra strength is, like the larger pelvis, designed to carry the extra burden of the unborn child. Concentrate upon these fundamental differences until you can set up an unmistakable male or female figure at will.

Note the black squares on the male skeleton. These are bony prominences where the bones are so near the surface that they affect the contour. When the body becomes fat, these spots become dimples or recessions in the surface. In thin or aged figures, these bones protrude.

Working from life or photographs will not eliminate the necessity of knowing anatomy and proportion. You should recognize what the humps and bumps are—and why they are there. Otherwise your drawing will have the look of inflated rubber, or a wax department-store dummy. The final work on any commission of importance should be drawn from a model or good copy of some kind, since it must compete with the work of men who use models and good copy. Most artists own and operate a camera as a help. But it will not do the whole job. Outlines traced from a photograph, because of the exaggerated foreshortening by the lenses, have a wide and dumpy look. Limbs look short and heavy. Hands and feet appear too large. If these distortions are not corrected, your drawing will simply look photographic.

It might be well to mention here some of the requirements of successful figure drawing. The "smart" female figure has some mannish contours. The shoulders are drawn a little wider than normal, without much slope, the hips a little narrower. The thighs and legs are made longer and more slender, with tapering calves. When the legs are together, they should touch at the thigh, knee, and ankle. The knees should be small. The leg is elongated from the knee down with small ankles. It is merely a waste of time to show an art director a figure that looks large-headed, narrow-shouldered, short-armed or -legged, wide-hipped, short, fat, dumpy, or pudgy. But a figure may be actually bony and unusually tall and still please a fashion editor.

Slimness in figure drawing has become almost a cult. What the artists of the Middle Ages considered voluptuous appeal would be plain fat today. Nothing will kill a sale so quickly as fatness or shortness. (It is a curious fact that short people are apt to draw short figures. A man with a short wife will tend to draw short women.) If my figures seem absurdly tall, remember that I am giving you the conception accepted as a standard. They will not look too tall to the art buyer. In fact, some of my figures here are even shorter than I would instinctively draw them.

The essence of successful male figure drawing is that it be kept masculine—plenty of bone and muscle. The face should be lean, the cheeks slightly hollowed, the eyebrows fairly thick (never in a thin line), the mouth full, the chin prominent and well defined. The figure is, of course, wide shouldered and at least six feet (eight or more heads) tall. Unfortunately, it is not easy to find these lean-faced, hard-muscled male models. They are usually at harder work.

Children should be drawn fairly close to the scale of proportions given in this book. Babies obviously should be plump, dimpled, and healthy. Special study should be given to the folds and creases at the neck, wrists, and ankles. The cheeks are full and round, the chin is well under. The upper lip protrudes somewhat. The nose is round and small and concave at the bridge. The ears are small, thick, and round. The eyes practically fill the openings. The hands are fat and dimpled and there is considerable taper to the short fingers. Until the structure of babies is well understood it is almost fatal to try to draw them without good working material.

Keep all children up to six or eight years quite chubby. From eight to twelve they can be drawn very much as they appear, though the relative size of the head should be a little larger than normal.

If you get into character drawing, you may do a fat fellow—but don't make him too young. Do not draw ears too large or protruding in any male drawing. The male hands should be exaggerated a little in size and in the ideal type must look bony and muscular. Soft, round hands on a man simply won't go.

The art director seldom points out your faults. He simply says he does not like your drawing. Any one of the above mistakes may account for his dislike. Ignorance of the demands upon you is as great a handicap as ignorance of anatomy.

MALE SKELETON, BACK AND SIDE VIEWS

SHOULDER
BACK VIEW

1 SCAPULA
2 HUMERUS
3 ULNA
4 RADIUS
5 CLAVICLE

1 PELVIS
2 SACRUM
3 FEMUR
4 PATELLA
5 TIBIA
6 FIBULA

SHOULDER, FRONT
1 CLAVICLE
2 SCAPULA
3 HUMERUS

PELVIS, BACK VIEW.

PECTORALIS MAJOR

1 PECTORALIS MINOR
2 BICEPS

SERRATUS MAGNUS

1 DELTOID
2 BICEPS
3 PECTORALIS MAJOR
4 LATISSIMUS DORSI
5 SERRATUS MAGNUS

1 STERNO MASTOID
2 TRAPEZIUS
3 STERNOHYOID

STERNOHYOID
STERNO MASTOID
TRAPEZIUS
DELTOID
PECTORALIS MAJOR
BICEPS
SERRATUS MAGNUS
RECTUS ABDOMINIS
EXTERNAL OBLIQUE
GLUTEUS MEDIUS
PSOAS ILIACUS
TENSOR FASCIAE LATAE
PECTINEUS
ADDUCTOR LONGUS
SARTORUS
GRACILIS
VASTUS LATERALIS
RECTUS FEMORIS
VASTUS MEDIALIS
BAND OF RICHTER
PATELLA
GASTROCNEMIUS (CALF)
TIBIA - (SHIN BONE)
TIBIALIS ANTICUS
PERONEUS LONGUS
SOLEUS

ERECTOR SPINAE
GROUP

SPLENIUS

TRAPEZIUS

DELTOID
INFRA SPINATUS
RHOMBOID
TERES MAJOR
LATISSIMUS DORSI

EXTERNAL OBLIQUE

GLUTEUS MEDIUS

GLUTEUS MAXIMUS

ILIOTIBIAL BAND

GRACILIS
SEMITENDINOSUS

BICEPS FEMORIS

GASTROCNEMIUS

PERONEUS LONGUS

TENDON OF ACHILLES
SOLEUS

1 ERECTOR SPINAE GROUP
2 RHOMBOID
3 LEVATOR ANGULI SCAPULI
4 TRAPEZIUS

BONES

1 SCAPULA
2 HUMERUS
3 ULNA
4 RADIUS

INTERNAL CONDYLE OF THE HUMERUS

* SHOWS ON OPPOSITE SIDE WHEN HAND IS TURNED OVER

HUMERUS

ULNA

KEY

1 DELTOID
2 BICEPS
3 TRICEPS, OUTER HEAD
3A   "   LONG   "
3B   "   INNER   "
4 BRACHIALIS ANTICUS
5 SUPINATOR LONGUS
6 EXTENSOR CARPI RADIALIS
7   "   'S COMMUNIS
8   "   'S OF THE THUMB
9 FLEXOR CARPI ULNARIS
10 PRONATOR TERES
11 FLEXOR CARPI RADIALIS
12 PALMARIS LONGUS
9 &13 FLEXOR CARPI ULNARIS
14 EXTENSOR CARPI ULNARIS
15 ANCONEUS
16 FLEXORS OF THE HAND
17 BRACHIORADIALIS

DRAW THESE ARMS
TO HELP FIX THEM
IN YOUR MEMORY

OUTER SIDE VIEW RIGHT ARM   INNER VIEW RIGHT ARM   UNDER AND INSIDE VIEW

INNER VIEW (BODY SIDE)   OUTER SIDE   BACK VIEW   BACK VIEW, PALM IN

PELVIS
SACRUM
FEMUR
PATELLA
TIBIA
FIBULA

STAY WITH IT!

MUSCLES OF THE LEG

1. PSOAS ILIACUS
2. PECTINEUS
3. ADDUCTOR MAGNUS
4. TIBIALIS ANTICUS
5. EXTENSOR LONGUS DIGITORUM
6. RECTUS FEMORIS
7. VASTUS LATERALIS
8. VASTUS MEDIALIS
9. GASTROCNEMIUS
10. SOLEUS

11. GRACILIS
12. TENSOR FASCIAE LATAE
13. GLUTEUS MEDIUS
14. ILIOTIBIAL BAND
15. BAND OF RICHTER
16. PATELLAR LIGAMENT
17. PERONEUS LONGUS
18. GLUTEUS MAXIMUS
19. SEMIMEMBRANOSUS
20. SEMITENDINOSUS

21 BICEPS FEMORIS
22 VASTUS INTERMEDIUS
23 SARTORIS
24 TENDON OF ACHILLES

MUSCLES OF THE LEG. BACK AND SIDE VIEW

BACK VIEW

OUTER SIDE VIEW

THERE IS NO OTHER WAY TO ACQUIRE A KNOWLEDGE OF ANATOMY THAN TO "DIG IT OUT". STAY WITH IT UNTIL YOU CAN DRAW THE MUSCLES FROM MEMORY. GET FURTHER BOOKS ON THE SUBJECT. THE AUTHOR RECOMMENDS THE BOOKS BY GEORGE BRIDGMAN AS EXCELLENT. THERE IS ALSO A VERY FINE BOOK OF DIAGRAMS, "ARTISTIC ANATOMY" BY WALTER F. MOSES. IN THESE BOOKS, THE SUBJECT IS MORE EXPERTLY COVERED, AND MUCH MORE COMPLETE. "IT PAYS TO KNOW", SO STAY WITH IT !

III. BLOCK FORMS, PLANES, FORESHORTENING, AND LIGHTING

The transition from outline and specific construction to the figure rendered in light and shadow is quite a hurdle. Often the student is unable to make this jump. The difficulty arises from a lack of conception of the solid. Yet there are intermediate steps that can make the rendering of the third dimension (thickness) fairly simple.

How can a solid form be set into space? How do we conceive of it so that we know it has bulk and weight—that we can pick it up or bump into it? The answer is that our eye instinctively recognizes the solid by the way light falls upon it. As far as the artist is concerned, when there is no light there is no form. The only reason an outline drawing can suggest the solid is that theoretically a drawing represents the form in a light that comes from directly behind the artist; hence the form casts no shadow visible to us. As the contours and edges turn away from us and the light, they tend to darken until they begin to look like lines, sharp at the edges and softening as they approach the middle or closer part of the form. We call this "flat lighting." It is the only way that form can be rendered without shadow, but it does include "halftone," which is the next step between the full light and the shadow. The shadow is really there also, but we cannot see it from our viewpoint.

When white paper is used for the drawing, the paper theoretically represents the greatest light—that is, the *plane which is at right angles to the source of light.* In all cases other than flat-front lighting, the form is rendered by the correct interpretation of the direction of the planes away from the right-angle planes, or the turning away of the form from the source of light.

The first and brightest planes are called the "light planes." The next planes are the "halftone planes," and the third planes, which are unable to receive direct lighting because of their angle, are called "shadow planes." Within the shadow planes may be those that are still receiving subdued, reflected light; these are called "planes of reflection." Form cannot be rendered without a clear grasp of this principle. The planes are worked out in the simple order of: (1) light, (2) halftone, (3) shadow—which is the darkest and is at the point where the plane parallels the direction of light, and (4) reflected light. This is called "simple lighting." It is unquestionably the best for our purpose. When there are several sources of light, the whole composition becomes a hodgepodge, inconsistent with natural light and highly confusing to the student. Sunlight naturally gives us the most perfect rendition of form. Daylight is softer and more diffused, but the principle still holds. Artificial light, unless controlled and based upon the sun principle, is the fly in the ointment. The camera may be able to get away with four or five sources of light; the chances are that the artist cannot.

Before you plunge into the intricacies of light and shadow, it would be well to know what is going to happen to form when light strikes it. Since the light can be made to come from any direction, the organization of the light-to-dark may start with any plane as the light plane. In other words, in a top lighting slightly to the front, the plane across the breast would be the light plane. Move the light to the side, and that plane would become a halftone plane. Set the light below, and the same plane is in shadow. Hence *all planes are relative to the light source.*

Let us start, then, with the form in the simplest possible terms. By drawing block forms we cut out the extreme subtleties of halftone. Continuing a plane as a single tone on a surface as long as we can before turning it in another direction is simplification, or massing. Actually the figure is very rounded. But rounded surfaces produce such a delicate gradation of light and shadow that it is difficult to approach without a simplification and massing of these tones. Strangely enough, the simplification is a good deal better in the end than the exact photographic and literal interpretation. It is somewhat like trying to paint a tree by painting every leaf instead of massing the foliage into its big forms and working for bulk rather than intricate detail.

After we have mastered the larger plane, we can soften it at its edges to mold it into the more rounded form, while retaining all we can of the bigness of conception. Or, we can start with a big block, as the sculptor would start with a block of stone or marble. We hew away the excess and block in the general mass that we want. We then subdivide the big, straight planes into smaller ones until the rounded effect has been produced. It is like going around a circle with a series of short, straight lines. You may question why we do not at once proceed to the finished, smooth, and round form. The answer is that in a drawing or painting, something of the individual procedure and structural quality should remain. When it is too much smoothed down and polished, it becomes entirely factual. The camera can do *that*. In a drawing, however, "finish" is not necessarily art. It is the interpretation and process of individual conception that is art and that has value. If you include all the literal facts and actualities, the result will be boring. It is your selection of relevant facts that will create interest. A sweeping conception carries with it vitality, purpose, and conviction. The more detailed and involved we get, the less

forceful and powerful is our message. We can take a compass and draw a circle perfectly, but we have left no trace of ourselves in what we have set down. It is the big form that does the job—not the little and the exact.

On pages 70 and 71 I have tried to give an inkling of what I mean. Here the surface is conceived of as having mass and bulk. The effect is sculptural. It is looking at our mannikin a little differently. If we are to compose the mannikin of simplified blocks, how shall we shape those blocks? Your way is as good as mine. Shape them any way you will to arrive at a massed or bulk effect. This is the real approach to "solidity" in your work: actually thinking of the mass, bulk, and weight of it.

With this approach, we take the art-store wooden mannikin and use it as a basis for setting up a figure (page 72). We go a step further with the mannikin on page 73 and attempt to eliminate the stiffness of the jointed parts, still thinking though in terms of masses.

Retaining these terms we take solids (page 74) and tip them, remembering at all times what each *section* of the mass would be and where it belongs in relation to the whole. We must depend chiefly upon line to render the form, or that part of it which goes back into space, as seen by the eye of the observer. This is foreshortening. Actual measurement of length cannot be made, since viewing the form from one point is like looking at a gun barrel aimed directly at you. We must think of the contours and form as sections lined up one behind the other. An outline is rarely sufficient, however, to represent the receding sections; most often halftone and shadow are needed as well, as shown on page 75. Pages 76 and 77 are an interpretation of the rounded figure flattened into planes that go a step further than our simplest block forms. On pages 78 and 79 we place the simplified form of the head under various kinds of lighting.

BLOCKING IN "FORM" IS THE FOUNDATION FOR ALL WORK RENDERED IN LIGHT AND SHADOW. TRY TO REDUCE THE FORM TO ITS SIMPLEST TERMS, ADDING WHATEVER DEGREE OF "FINISH" YOU WISH. REMEMBER, A SIMPLE CLEAN CUT STATEMENT IS BETTER THAN SAYING TOO MUCH. ANATOMY IS STUDIED FIRST TO HELP YOU BUILD SIMPLE FORMS CONVINCINGLY. A MANNIKIN WILL HELP YOU NOW, OR SOME CASTS. YOU NEED NOT, AT THIS STAGE, ATTEMPT LIGHT AND SHADOW, IF IT'S TOO DIFFICULT. JUST DRAW BIG BLOCKY SHAPES. TRY TO SENSE THE FORM ALL THE WAY ROUND. THE OBJECT IS "TO GET OUT OF THE FLAT INTO THE SOLID".

SKETCH THE MANNIKIN

THEN BUILD YOUR FIGURE

WHEN USED WITH A BIT OF
ANATOMICAL KNOWLEDGE
THE WOODEN MANNIKIN
CAN BE A GREAT HELP IN
MAKING PRELIMINARY
SKETCHES, LAYOUTS AND
COMPOSITIONS.
YOUR ART DEALER MAY
HAVE ONE OR CAN GET IT
FOR YOU.

THIS CAN BE
REAL FUN!

FORESHORTENING

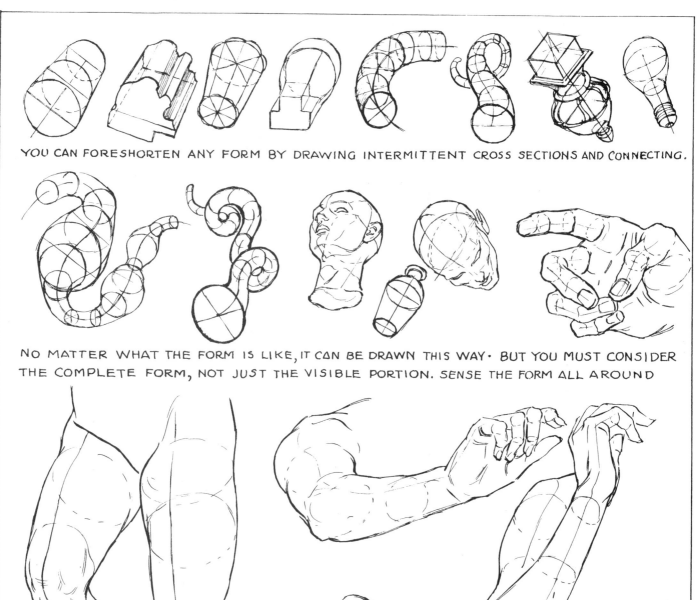

YOU CAN FORESHORTEN ANY FORM BY DRAWING INTERMITTENT CROSS SECTIONS AND CONNECTING.

NO MATTER WHAT THE FORM IS LIKE, IT CAN BE DRAWN THIS WAY. BUT YOU MUST CONSIDER THE COMPLETE FORM, NOT JUST THE VISIBLE PORTION. SENSE THE FORM ALL AROUND

THE CONTOURS PASS IN FRONT, OR OVER ONE ANOTHER. YOU SHOULD PRACTICE FROM LIFE OR GOOD PHOTOGRAPHS.

PLANES

PLANES ARE THEORETICAL FLATTENING OF ROUNDED FORMS AS WELL AS ACTUAL FLAT AREAS. IN ART AN EXTREME SMOOTHNESS AND ROUNDNESS OF FORM TENDS TOWARD THE "SLICK" AND "PHOTOGRAPHIC." IT SHOULD BE AVOIDED "LIKE THE MEASLES."

THE USE OF PLANES GIVES MORE OF AN INDIVIDUAL QUALITY. NO TWO ARTISTS WILL SEE PLANES ALIKE. "SQUARENESS" OF ROUNDED FORM IMPARTS A CERTAIN RUGGEDNESS AND VITALITY. A GOOD AXIOM IS, "SEE HOW SQUARE YOU CAN MAKE THE ROUND."

HERE IS A ROUND FORM SET INTO "PLANES" OR AREAS OF LIGHT HALFTONE AND SHADOW.

(DIRECTION OF LIGHT)

THERE IS NO SET RULE FOR PLANES. YOU DRAW THEM AS YOU THINK BEST TO SUIT THE SUBJECT.

THE "LIGHT" PLANES ARE THOSE IN FULL LIGHT. THE "HALFTONE" PLANES ARE THOSE IN HALF LIGHT. THE "PASSAGE TONE" IS THAT WHICH MERGES THE HALF-TONE AND SHADOW. THE "REFLECT" IS THE LIGHTEST TONE IN THE SHADOW.

HERE WE HAVE "SQUARED" THE ROUNDED FIGURE INTO PLANES. THE PURPOSE IS TO USE THEM AS A BASIS FOR RENDERING LIGHT, HALFTONE AND SHADOW, IN THE SIMPLEST TERMS AND AT THE SAME TIME PRESERVING THE MAIN STRUCTURAL FORMS. WE THEN "SOFTEN" THE EDGES OF THE PLANES TO THE DEGREE THAT WE DEEM SATISFACTORY.

PLANES ARE A "PRELIMINARY CARVING" OF THE SURFACE FORM.

PLANES

THERE IS NO SET OF PLANES WHICH WILL FIT THE FIGURE AT ALL TIMES, SINCE THE SURFACE FORM CHANGES WITH MOVEMENT SUCH AS BENDING AT THE WAIST, MOVEMENT OF THE SHOULDERS, ETC. THE PLANES ARE GIVEN MAINLY TO SHOW HOW THE FORMS CAN BE SIMPLIFIED · EVEN WHEN YOU HAVE THE LIVE MODEL OR COPY, YOU STILL WORK FOR THE MAIN PLANES OF LIGHT, HALFTONE AND SHADOW · OTHERWISE YOU MAY HAVE AN OVERPOWERING CONFUSION OF TONES.

REMEMBER !

WHEN WORKING WITHOUT A MODEL OR COPY, YOU DRAW THE PLANES FOR THE LIGHT, HALFTONE AND SHADOW · WHEN WORKING WITH THE MODEL OR COPY, YOU DRAW THE PLANES FROM THE LIGHT, HALFTONE AND SHADOW.

LIGHTING

1. "FLAT LIGHTING "-(FROM DIRECTLY IN FRONT) GOOD FOR POSTER, DECORATIVE, SIMPLICITY.

2. "STAGE "- DRAMATIC, WEIRD, GHOSTLY, LIKE THE LIGHT FROM A CRATER. (LOW FRONT)

3. "3/4 SIDE "- A GOOD LIGHTING. PLACE THE LIGHT 45° FRONT. USE ONE LIGHT ONLY.

4. "3/4 TOP SIDE "- ONE OF THE BEST. IT GIVES MAXIMUM LIGHT, HALFTONE, SHADOW & REFLECT.

5. "TOP "- A VERY BEAUTIFUL LIGHTING. THIS GIVES GREAT LUMINOSITY TO SHADOWS.

6. "TOP BACK "- WITH REFLECTOR, VERY GOOD. GIVES GREAT SOLIDITY TO THE FORM.

7. "CRISSCROSS "- USUALLY BAD. NEVER HAVE LIGHT EQUAL ON BOTH SIDES. CUTS UP FORM.

8. "ALL FLAT "- PROVING HOW EXCESS LIGHTS MAY ACTUALLY ELIMINATE SOLID FORM.

9. "½ and ½ " BAD. AREAS OF LIGHT & SHADOW SHOULD NEVER BE EQUAL. GIVE ONE THE EDGE.

Here the camera lends us a helping hand by showing the "actual" light as it falls on a simplified form. The form has been rounded to give you the gradation from light through halftone to shadow. Number 1 is a front lighting, corresponding to the treatment of a flat and unshaded outline drawing. The only shadow, under the chin, occurs because the light was raised a little to allow the camera to be placed under it. Camera and light, of course, could not have been placed in the identical spot. Had this been possible, there would have been no shadow. An all-flat or formless lighting may be obtained by piling in equal lighting from every direction (Number 8).

When there is a single source of light on the object, the shadowed side reflects some of the light in a luminous manner. The reflected-light areas within the shadow, however, never become competitive with the areas in light, and the unity of the mass of light as opposed to the mass of shadow is maintained. In drawing nothing within a shadow area should ever be as light as that within a light area, because reflected light is never so strong as its source. One exception might be the use of a mirror. That, however, would be a duplication of the light source rather than reflection (refraction). The dazzling light upon water is another example of refraction.

Simple lighting, which means lighting from a single source, and the reflected light of that source, is the most perfect lighting there is. It renders form in its actual contours and bulk. True modeling of form cannot be approached any other way, since to change the normal or true value of the plane is to change and upset the form; if the value is "off," the form is incorrect. Since the photographer may not have reasoned this out, it is better to make your own photographs, or at least supervise the lighting of any photographic copy. The photographer hates shadows; the artist loves them.

LIGHT BACKGROUND

10. "SILHOUETTE" - THE REVERSE OF NO. 1. GOOD FOR POSTER, DESIGN & FLAT EFFECTS.

DARK BACKGROUND

11. "FRINGE" - LIGHTED DIRECTLY FROM BACK SLIGHTLY TOP. VERY EFFECTIVE.

DARK BACKGROUND.

12. "SKY". TOP WITH A LIGHT GROUND FOR REFLECTION. NATURAL, VERY GOOD.

DRAW SHADOWS FIRST, THEN HALFTONES.
CAST SHADOWS ARE DARKEST. DO NOT
MAKE FORM SHADOWS TOO BLACK.
MODEL FROM SHADOW TO THE LIGHT.
KEEP ALL HALFTONES LIGHTER THAN
SHADOWS. DON'T "OVER MODEL" LIGHT.

☐ LIGHT (PAPER)
☰ HALFTONE
☰ SHADOW

The simplest way to explain the fundamental principle of rendering light and shadow is to think of a ball with light focused upon it just as the sun lights the earth. The area on the ball closest to the light is the high light (A), comparable to noon. If we move on the surface of the sphere away from the high light in any direction, we find that the light begins imperceptibly to fade into the halftone area (B), which may be compared to twilight, and then to last light (B+), and on to night (C). If there is nothing to reflect the light, there is true darkness; however, if the moon, a reflector of the sun's light, comes up, it will reflect light into the shadow (D). When light is intercepted by a body, its silhouette falls upon the adjacent light plane. This, the darkest of the shadows, is called "cast shadow." It is still possible, however, for a cast shadow to pick up some reflected light.

The artist should be able to look at any given place on his subject and determine to which area it belongs — the light, the halftone, the shadow, or the reflected light. Correct values must be given in order to obtain unity and organization of these four fundamental areas. Otherwise a drawing will not hold together. Treatment of light gives a drawing cohesion no less than structural form.

There are many things you can learn from photographs if you use them intelligently. Remember, however, that the range of light to dark is much greater in the eye than in pigment. You cannot possibly put down the full range; you have to simplify.

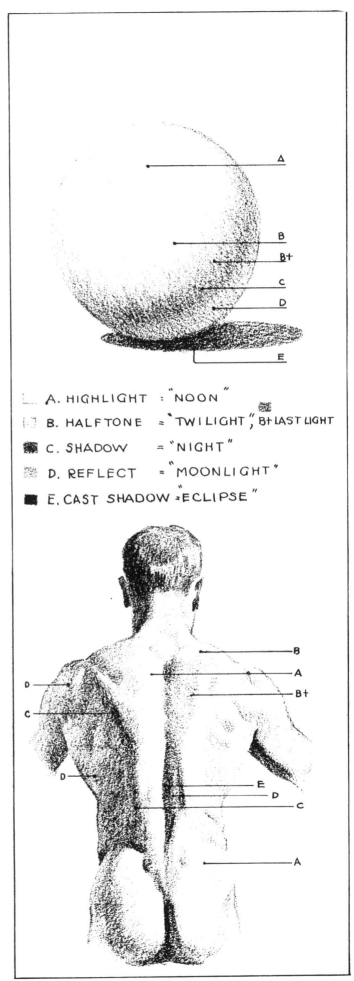

A. HIGHLIGHT = "NOON"

B. HALFTONE = "TWILIGHT", B+ LAST LIGHT

C. SHADOW = "NIGHT"

D. REFLECT = "MOONLIGHT"

E. CAST SHADOW = "ECLIPSE"

IV. DRAWING THE LIVE FIGURE: METHODS OF PROCEDURE

Before you undertake to draw from the living model, be sure you have absorbed all the preliminaries so far discussed. These are:

The proportions of the idealized figure
The general framework
The relationship of perspective to the figure
Movement and action
The mannikin and simplified building of the form
The anatomic construction
The planes by which we build light and shadow
Foreshortening
The fundamentals of light and shadow
The true modeling of form

Now when you have to draw something set up in front of you, you must possess still another fundamental skill—intelligent measurement. I say "intelligent" because your aim is not mere duplication.

Suppose you begin to draw a husky young man, arms uplifted, whom you want to interpret in terms of light, halftone, and shadow. You have set your light source low and to the right, so that there will be a varied play of light across the form. First, look for the area of greatest light. It is found on the chest under the left arm of the model. Now look for the whole mass of light as opposed to the whole mass of shadow. Sketch in the contours of the figure and block in these masses. (On page 83 you will find the halftones added and the shadows relatively darkened.) I suggest that you use the point of your pencil for the contours and the side of the lead for the massing of the halftone and shadow. When you are drawing with a pen, shadows and halftones can be achieved only by combinations of lines. But a brush or pencil adapts itself to mass. Observe, too, that the grain of your paper will add to or detract from the attractiveness of the texture of the drawing. Because of the method of reproduction, a coated, smooth paper could not be used for the drawings in this book. Beautiful grays and darks are possible, however, on the smooth papers if the side of a soft lead pencil is used. The halftones and darks may be produced in either pencil or charcoal by rubbing with the finger or a stump of paper. The whole figure drawing may be rubbed with a rag and the lights picked out with a kneaded eraser.

On pages 86 and 87, look over my shoulder as I proceed with my own method for drawing a figure. On page 88 see a plan of approach that I call the "visual survey." It is less complicated than it looks, for I have included visual measurement lines that, ordinarily, are not set down. It is a plan of finding level points and plumb points and the angles established by sighting a continuation of the line to see where it emerges. This is the only plan I know that can be depended upon to offer any degree of accuracy in freehand drawing.

It is easiest to sight in vertical and horizontal lines, so that important points directly across or under each other are quickly "checked." When a point falls outside the figure, such as a hand, angles of points within the figure will help to find it. When you have correctly placed one point, proceed to others, and finally your drawing will check with the model. This principle, also illustrated on page 89, applies to any subject before you and provides a valuable means of corroborating the accuracy of your drawing.

A

E

E

A

D

A

C

E

C

B

C

WHEN DRAWING FROM
LIFE OR PHOTOS, DRAW
THE CONTOURS OF THE
HALFTONE AND SHADOW
MASSES. STUDY ALL THE
SURFACE AREAS AND DE-
CIDE TO WHAT CLASS
EACH AREA BELONGS.
IS IT LIGHT, HALFTONE,
SHADOW, REFLECT OR
CAST SHADOW?

A LIGHT
B HALFTONE
B+ DK. HALFTONE
C SHADOW
D REFLECT
E CAST SHADOW

FIRST STAGE

LAST STAGE

THE VALUES WORKED
OUT. A DRAWING MAY
BE "STOPPED" BEFORE
ENTIRELY FINISHED.
SOMETIMES WHEN A
DRAWING "SUGGESTS"
ONLY, IT IS FAR MORE
INTERESTING.

USE THE SIDE OF THE
PENCIL FOR DRAWING
TONES OR VALUES, AND
A SHARP POINT FOR THE
CONTOURS.

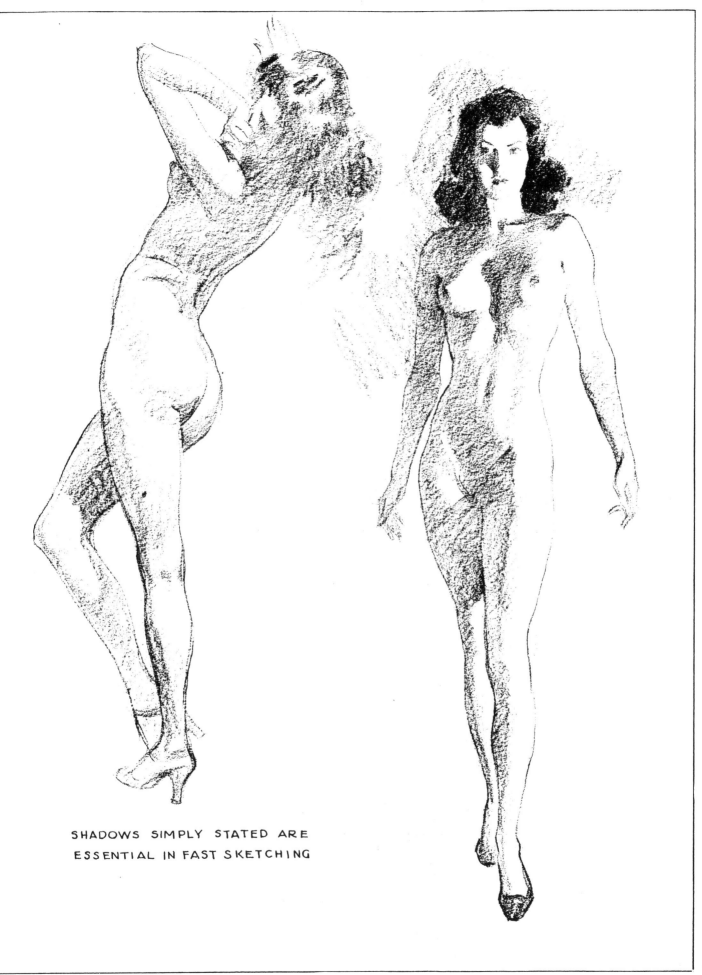

SHADOWS SIMPLY STATED ARE
ESSENTIAL IN FAST SKETCHING

MEASURE BY HOLDING PENCIL
ALWAYS AT ARM'S LENGTH

MEASURING THE SUBJECT

1. Establish two points on your paper as the desired height of pose (top and bottom). Draw a perpendicular through these points as the middle line of subject.

2. Locate the middle point of line (½). Now, holding pencil at arm's length, find the middle point on the subject before you. From the middle point get quarter points (up and down).

3. Take the greatest width of the pose. Compare it to the height. In my drawing it comes just above the right kneecap (about ⅓). Lay the width equally on each side of your middle point up and down. Now locate the middle point crossways on your model.

4. Your two lines will cross at this point. It is the middle point of your subject. *Remember this point on the model.*
You work out from it in all directions.

5. Now, with plumb line, or eye, locate all the important points that fall beneath one another. (In my drawing the subject's right heel was directly underneath her hair at the forehead, the knee under the nipple, etc.)

6. Start by blocking in head and torso and, from the head, sight straight up and down and straight across, all the way up and down the figure.

7. For the angles, sight straight on through and establish a point on the line where it falls under a known point. (See line of chest and nipples. The known point is the nose. This locates right nipple.)

8. If you constantly check points opposite, points underneath, and where the angles emerge, after having established height, width, and division points—your drawing will be accurate, and you will know it is!

LEVEL POINTS
PLUMB POINTS

PLUMB LINE

MAKE A "FINDER"

REMEMBER THIS PLAN GIVES THE ACTUAL LIVE PRO-PORTIONS. MAKE ANY ADJUSTMENTS YOU WISH AS YOU GO ALONG. USUALLY ADD A LITTLE IN LENGTH.

CUT TWO RIGHT ANGLES FROM SOME STIFF CARDBOARD, MARK OFF IN INCHES AND CLIP TOGETHER. THIS CAN BE ADJUSTED. IT GIVES PROPORTIONATE WIDTH TO HEIGHT.

V. THE STANDING FIGURE

Much of the essential equipment for professional figure drawing is described in the preceding chapters. You have now learned a "means of expression," but your use of that knowledge is just beginning. From this point onward you must learn to express yourself individually, showing your particular taste in the selection of models, choice of pose, dramatic sense and interpretation, characterization, and technical rendering.

Routine knowledge and fact thus become the basis for what is often referred to as inspiration, or spiritual quality, subjects that are little discussed in art textbooks. The truth is that there are no hard-and-fast rules. The best advice is to watch for the individual spark and fan it into flame when you find it. For my part, I have found that most students possess initiative, are open to suggestion, and are thoroughly capable of being inspired to express themselves ably. I believe that when the qualities necessary for acceptable drawing are pointed out, you may be helped tremendously to bridge the gap between amateur and professional drawing.

Two broad approaches are needed: First is the conception, or "What have you to say?" Second is the interpretation, or "How can you say it?" Both call for feeling and individual expression. Both call for initiative, knowledge, and inventiveness.

Let us take the first step. Before you pick up your pencil, or take a photograph, or hire a model, you must understand your problem and its purpose. You must search for an idea and interpret it. If the job at hand requires a drawing designed to sell something, ask yourself the following: To whom must this drawing appeal? Shall it be directed toward a selected or general class of buyer? Are the buyers going to be men or women? Is there a dramatic way of expressing the subject? Will a head or whole figure best serve to emphasize the idea? Should several figures make up the composition? Will a setting and locale help or can the message be conveyed better without these? Where and how will it be reproduced—newspaper, magazine, poster? You must take into account which advertising medium is to be used. A billboard, for example, will require a simple, flat background and the use of large heads, since the message must be taken in at a glance. Newspaper drawings should be planned for reproduction on cheap paper—i.e., line or simple treatment without subtlety in the halftone. For the magazine, where the reader has more time, you may use the complete figure and even background, if needed. The tendency, however, is to simplify and to strip drawings of all that is not of major importance.

With the second step you advance to the practical interpretation of the idea. Eliminate what you know to be impractical. For instance, do not approach a billboard subject with several complete figures, for their expressions will not carry from a distance. Granting, then, that you rightly choose large heads, what are the types you want? What are the expressions? What are the poses? Can you do better if you get out your camera and nail down an expression that you know cannot be held by the hour? Can you put Mother over here and have room for the lettering also? Would she be better over there? What will you choose for a background? What will be the style and color of her dress? You begin, at this point, to experiment with thumbnail impressions on a tissue pad until you can say, "That's it," and then, with all the vigor that is in you, proceed to prove that "that's it."

There is no book in the world that will do a job for you. There is no art director who can do your job. Even though the art director may go so far as to lay out the general idea, space, and placement, he still is asking for your interpretation. Again, there is no piece of copy that you can lay down in front of you which will completely answer your needs. Another man's work was done for his own purpose and for another problem. The principal difference between the amateur and the professional is that the latter courageously strikes out in his own way, while the former gropes for a way of expressing himself.

Endless variety in posing is possible. People stand up, kneel or crouch, sit or lie down; but there are a thousand ways of doing these things. It is surprising, for example, to observe how many ways there are in which to stand up.

Plan the standing figure carefully, remembering that, although standing still is a static pose, you can suggest that the standing figure is capable of movement. Only when you portray a tense moment demanding rigidity in the figure do you arrest the latent movement. To relieve the static feeling, put the weight on one leg, turn the torso, tip and turn the head, or allow the figure to lean upon or be supported by something. A fairly good rule is never to have face and eyes looking straight ahead and set squarely on the shoulders, unless you are trying for a definite "straight-from-the-shoulder attitude" to suggest defiance, impudence, or a pitting of one personality against another. This attitude reminds one too much of the old photographs in which Grandpa's head was held in a clamp during the process of getting his likeness.

See that either head or shoulders are turned or tipped, or both. With the standing figure everything is relaxation, balance, and a distribution of weight. Any sort of gesture is a relief from hands hanging motionless at the sides. A self-conscious girl has the feeling that she never knows what to do with her hands. The unimaginative artist, too, does not know what to do with the hands of his figures. But the girl can put her hands on her hips, finger her beads, fix her hair, pull out her vanity case, apply lipstick, smoke a cigarette. Hands can be most expressive.

If you show legs, let them be interesting even in the standing pose. Drop one knee. Raise a heel. Do anything except keep them glued to the floor side by side. Twist the body, drop one hip, get the elbows at different levels, clasp the hands, put one hand up to the face, do anything that keeps your drawing from looking like a wooden dummy. Draw a lot of little "funnies" until you find one that is interesting. *Make every standing figure do something beside just standing.* There are so many natural gestures possible, to combine with the telling of a story, to express an idea or emotion, that it should not be hard to be original.

When I illustrate a story, I usually read significant parts of the manuscript to the models. I try to get them to act out situations as naturally as possible. At the same time I try to think of how I would act under the circumstances in the story. There is, of course, the danger of overacting, or of using gestures that go beyond the natural or logical, which is almost as bad as being static.

Experiment with the lighting on the model to express best what you have in mind. Give importance to a portion of the figure by getting the strongest and most concentrated light upon it. Sometimes parts of a figure can be lost in shadow to advantage. Sometimes a silhouette may be stronger and more compelling than a brightly lighted subject.

The whole gamut of expression is there for you to choose from. Don't form a few habits that you continually repeat. Try to make each thing you do just as original in conception and execution as you possibly can.

SHADOW DEFINES FORM

DRAW THE SHAPES OF
THE LIGHT, HALFTONE,
AND SHADOW AREAS
AS CAREFULLY AS THE
CONTOURS.

FILL IN THE SHAPES
WITH THE RIGHT TONES
AND THE FORM TAKES
CARE OF ITSELF.

USE THE SAME PLAN
EVEN IN "QUICKIES"

THE MOST CERTAIN WAY TO LEARN TO
DRAW THE FIGURE IS TO START WITH
THE SKELETON, BUILDING IN THE BONES
AND THEN THE MAIN MUSCLES OVER THE
BONES. YOU CAN START WITH COPY
OF ANY FIGURE, OR A MODEL. MANY
PROFESSIONAL ARTISTS BUILD UP
THEIR FIGURES BEFORE ADDING THE
CLOTHING. TRY IT WITH VERY SIMPLE
POSES AT FIRST. EVENTUALLY THE BONES
AND MUSCLES WILL BECOME INSTINCT
AS YOU DRAW. YOU WILL SEE THEM
AS PLANES OF LIGHT, HALFTONE AND
SHADOW. KNOW THAT IT IS APPARENT
TO ANY ARTIST WHO KNOWS ANATOMY
WHEN THE OTHER FELLOW DOES NOT.
BE ONE WHO KNOWS. THE STRUGGLE IS
TOO HARD ANYWAY TO ADD THE HANDI-
CAP OF NOT KNOWING. YOUR TIME
WILL BE TOO PRECIOUS TO HAVE TO
STRUGGLE WITH CONSTRUCTION, AS
WELL AS ALL THE OTHER THINGS.

DO YOU KNOW YOUR MUSCLES?
LET'S FIND OUT, TO BE SURE.

WRITE IN THE NAMES OF THE MUSCLES
THEN REFER BACK TO YOUR ANATOMY
AND SEE IF YOU WERE CORRECT.
IF YOU CAN'T DO IT, YOU NEED MORE
STUDY. GO BACK AND GET IT THIS TIME.
YOU WILL NEVER BE SORRY!

A typical problem worked out with an advertising art director:

"Please rough out some little figures for pose only," an art director says to you, "to show to the Blank Knitting Company, suggesting our next ad. Indicate a one-piece bathing suit. Details of the bathing suit will be supplied later. Use a standing pose. The figure will be cut out against a white background, and the ad is to occupy a half page up and down in the Satevepost."

When you have made a series of roughs, show the two you like best to the art director, who takes them to his client. Afterward the art director tells you, "Mr. Blank likes these. Please draw them actual size for the magazine. The page size is nine-and-three-eighths by twelve-and-one-eighth inches. You are to have the left half of the page up and down. Pencil will do. Use light and shadow on the figure."

Mr. Blank O.K.'s one of your pencil sketches, and the art director says, "Get your model and take some snaps. Our client wants outdoor sunlit lighting and cautions us against getting a squint in the model's eyes."

The next step is to photograph a friend in a bathing suit. The chances are you will have to idealize her figure when you make your drawing from this photograph. Make her eight heads tall. Raise the crotch to the middle of the figure. Trim the hips and thighs if necessary.

She might be smiling over her shoulder at you. Have her hair blowing, perhaps. Find some use for the hands. Make the whole drawing as appealing as possible.

Since your drawing will be reproduced by halftone engraving, you have a full range of values with which to work. You may use pencil, charcoal, litho pencil, Wolff pencil, or wash. You can rub if you prefer. You also have the choice of pen and ink, brush, or drybrush. The drawing should be made on Bristol or illustration board and should be kept flat. Never roll a drawing that is to be reproduced.

VI. THE FIGURE IN ACTION: TURNING AND TWISTING

Every good action pose should have a suggestion of "sweep." Perhaps I can best describe sweep by saying that the movement which immediately precedes the pose is still felt. On the following pages I have tried to show this sweep or the line that the limbs have just followed. The cartoonist can add terrifically to the sense of motion by drawing his sweep with lines back of a moving hand or foot.

The only way to get sweep in the line is to have your model go through the entire movement and observe it carefully, choosing the instant that suggests the most movement. Usually the action can be best expressed if you use the start or finish of the sweep. A baseball pitcher suggests the most action either as he is all wound up, ready to throw, or just as he lets go of the ball. A golfer expresses movement best at the start or finish of the swing. If you were to show him on the point of hitting the ball, your drawing would have no action pictorially, and he would appear only to be addressing the ball in his ordinary stance. A horse seems to be going faster when his legs are either all drawn up under him or fully extended. The pendulum of a clock appears to be moving when it is at either extreme of its swing. A hammer raised from a nail suggests a harder blow and more movement than if it were shown close to the nail.

For psychological effect in drawing, it is essential to acquire the full range of movement. The observer must be made to complete the full motion, or to sense the motion that has just been completed. You would instinctively duck from a fist drawn 'way back from your face, whereas you might not withdraw at all from a fist two inches away. The prize fighter has learned to make good use of this psychology in his short punches.

Another means of illustrating action is to show its result or effect, as, for instance, a glass that has fallen over and spilled its contents, with an arm or hand just above it. The actual movement has been completed. Another example is that of a man who has fallen down after a blow, with the arm that hit him still extended.

There are instances, however, when the middle of the action is best. This is called "suspended action." A horse in the act of clearing a fence, a diver in mid-air, a building collapsing— are all examples of suspended action.

Fix in your mind the whole sweep of action and make little sketches at this point. At times you can help the action with a bit of blur, some dust, a facial expression. The cartoonist can write in, "Swish," "Smack," "Zowie," "Bing," "Crash," but you may not.

If you perform the action, it helps to give you the feel of it. Get up and do it, even if it does seem a little silly. If you can study the action in front of a large mirror, so much the better. There should be a mirror in every studio.

Some of your "action" camera shots may be disappointing unless you keep these facts in mind; knowing them helps you click the shutter at the precise moment.

FOLLOW THE SHADOW DOWN
WITH THE SIDE OF THE LEAD.

THIS IS A QUICK AND SIMPLE WAY OF
RENDERING, PEN OUTLINE WITH THE SIDE
OF THE PENCIL LEAD FOR SHADING. THIS
WAS DRAWN ON "BAINBRIDGE COQUILLE 2"

PEN AND PENCIL QUICK SKETCHES
ARE EFFECTIVE FOR ROUGHS, LAYOUTS
OR COMPOSITIONS TO BE SUBMITTED.

A TYPICAL PROBLEM

A typical problem worked out with an art editor of a fiction magazine:

The art editor says, "I have picked for illustration this paragraph from the manuscript":

" 'The last act was over. Jackie was removing the scant costume she had worn in the final chorus. She was alone in her dressing-room, or so she thought, until, by some inexplicable instinct, she turned quickly toward the jumble of costumes hanging in her wardrobe. There was unmistakable movement in the glitter of sequins.' "

"Now," continues the editor, "I'd like to see a rough or two in pencil on this before you go ahead. I think we can use a vignette shape better than a rectangular picture. Take about two-thirds of the page. The girl should be featured, bringing her up large in the space. We want something with action and punch and sex appeal but nothing offensive. Very little background necessary—just enough to place her. The girl, you know, has black hair and is tall, slender, and beautiful."

Proceed to make several roughs or thumbnail sketches for your own approval. It is clear that the girl is frightened and has been caught off guard. Someone is hiding—a rather sinister situation. The emotion to communicate and dramatize is fear. The story says she turned quickly, and that she was removing her scant costume, and the editor has said there must be nothing offensive in the drawing. You must put across the fact that she is in a dressing-room at the theater. A bit of the dressing table and mirror might be shown, and, of course, the closet or wardrobe where the intruder is hiding.

Project yourself into the situation and imagine her gesture, the sweep of movement. She might have pulled off a slipper, looking around with a startled expression. Perhaps the hands can do something to emphasize fear.

To get an idea of a chorus costume, go to a movie of a musical comedy. Look up some clips of chorus girls. After you have decided on a pose or arrangement of the subject, get someone to pose for some studies or snaps. Use a photo flood lamp. Plan the light as though it were the only light in the room, shining over the dressing-table. You can get dramatic effects with your lighting. Go at the problem as seriously as though it were an actual commission, for if it does become a reality, you will have to be ready for it. You cannot start being an illustrator with your first job. You will have to be judged an illustrator before you can get the assignment.

Take a paragraph from any magazine story and do your version of an illustration for it. Better, take one that was not illustrated by another artist, or, if it was, forget entirely his interpretation and style. *Don't under any circumstances copy another illustrator and submit the result as your own drawing.*

After you have read this book, come back to this page and try the illustration again. Save your drawings for samples.

The paragraph quoted for illustration is, of course, fictitious. The art director's demands, however, are altogether real. Most magazines pick the situation. Some even send you layouts for arrangement, for space filling, text space, et cetera. All send the manuscript for you to digest. Some ask you to pick the spots and show them roughs first. Most like to see what they are going to get before you do the final drawings. You may work in any medium for black and white half-tone reproduction.

VII. FORWARD MOVEMENT: THE TIPPED LINE OF BALANCE

The theory of depicting forward movement (any action that carries the whole body forward) requires that the top always be shown ahead of the base. If you balance a pole on your hand, you must follow with your hand the movement of the top of the pole. If it leans in any direction and you move the base in the same direction at the same speed, the pole maintains a constant slant between base and top. And the faster it goes the greater the slant.

So with figures in forward movement. A line drawn down through the middle of the forward-moving figure will slant exactly as the pole does. If you think of a picket fence with all the palings slanted and parallel, instead of vertical, you have a clear idea of the line of balance in forward movement. On pages 118 and 119 is a series of pictures taken with a fast lens, for the motion picture camera is actually too slow to stop movement for "still" reproduction and enlargement. The separate shots were taken at split seconds apart and pieced together to show the progression of the movement. I wished particularly to have the figure remain the same size throughout the sequence. The photographs reveal many facts, not apparent to the naked eye, about what takes place in the acts of running or walking.

In walking or running, the line of balance remains a constant forward slant as long as the same speed is maintained and tips more as the speed is increased. This change is hard to see because the moving arms and legs distract one's attention from the action. A person must lean the body forward to take a normal step. The balance is caught by the forward foot. The forward push comes from the foot in back. The arms move in reverse of the legs, so that, when the left leg goes forward, the left arm goes back. The center of the stride expresses the least movement. Note the last picture on page 119. For this photograph my model stood still and tried to pose as if he were moving. You will see at once how unconvincing the motion is. It is not the fault of the model but the fact that the important principle of forward movement is not working in the pose. Movement drawn without consideration for the tipped line of balance will not give the impression of forward movement. The drawing, no matter how anatomically correct, will resemble the movement of a jumping-jack suspended from a string.

The tipped line may be placed lightly on your paper and the figure built upon it. Technically, a heel should never be placed directly under the head but in back of it, to give motion. The foot that is carrying the weight and pushing should always be in back of the line of balance.

We think of the act of walking as if the foot describes an arc with the hip as center. What actually happens is that the hip describes the arc with the foot as center. Each step is a center with a fanlike movement going on above it. The foot that is *off* the ground swings in an arc forward from the hip, whereas the foot *on* the ground reverses the arc. As we walk along, what happens is this: foot moves body, body moves foot, foot moves body, body moves foot. Each leg takes the job over as soon as it is put on the ground, and the other leg relaxes and swings forward, mostly by momentum, until it takes over. Both actions go on simultaneously.

Hip and knee drop on the relaxed side. The leg carrying the weight is straight as it passes under the hip and bends at the knee as the heel comes up. Photographs illustrate this clearly. The relaxed leg is bent at the knee as it swings forward. It does not straighten out until after it has passed the other knee. This is very well defined in the side views of the walking poses. The legs are both fairly straight at the extremes of the stride. Here again is that paradox, that the legs seem to express most motion at the start or finish of the sweep described in the last chapter. Note particularly how much the girl's flying hair adds to the movement in the running poses. Also, the girl runs with arms bent, although in walking they swing naturally as they hang down.

Try to base walking and running poses on photos of actual movement. They are well worth obtaining—and those given here will prove valuable for reference in a pinch. To get all the action that is in a stride would require a slow-motion sequence, with page after page of pictures reproduced to any practical size. I feel this is hardly necessary; careful study of the two following pages should suffice.

Start drawing mannikin poses. See if you can, in a series of small framework sketches, draw all the way through a complete stride. In drawing back views of walking poses, remember that the pushing leg in back of the figure is straight until the heel leaves the ground, the heel and toes being lifted by the bending knee.

The use of cameras by artists is a controversial subject. Yet the demands on the present-day artist for action, expression, and dramatic interpretation are so exacting that it seems a bit ridiculous to fake these things when the actual knowledge is so easy to obtain by means of a camera. I do not admire a photographic-looking drawing, but I certainly detest a drawing that is meant to have virility and conviction but is inane and static through ignorance or laziness on the part of the artist. The fact that you can learn things of value from the camera is reason enough for you, as an artist, to have and use one.

The source of your knowledge, as mentioned before, is immaterial. Why put a model through the ordeal of trying to keep a vivacious smile on by the hour? No one can hold such a pose. We can learn more about a smile from the camera in five minutes than we can in five years of trying to "catch" it with the eye alone. Limbs move too fast for the naked eye to record. Expressions change and are gone in an instant. The camera is the one means of nailing these down so that we can study them by the hour. It is an unpardonable sin merely to copy. If you have nothing of your own to add, have no feeling about it, and are satisfied, technically, with the manner of treatment and have no desire to change this, then throw away your pencils and brushes and use the camera only. There will be many instances where you won't know what else to do but to copy, but these instances will be fewer as you try to express what you feel and like through your increasing technical knowledge.

Use your camera for all it's worth as part of your equipment. But keep it as equipment—not the end, but a means, just as your knowledge of anatomy is a means. Every successful artist whom I know, though it may be heresy to say so, has a camera and uses it. Many artists I know are expert photographers, taking their own pictures and developing them. Most use the small or candid variety of camera and enlarge their prints. The camera broadens their scope tremendously in securing data outside the studio. Start saving for a camera right now if you have not already made it one of your "means."

Going on with our line of balance, there are times when this line may be curved. In a sense, then, the line of balance is like a spring. For instance, a figure may be pushing very hard against something. The pushing would bend his figure backward. Again, if he were pulling hard, it would bend the figure the other way. Dancing poses can be built on the curved line, as well as swaying figures. Movement can be straight as an arrow, or curved like the path of a skyrocket. Either suggests powerful motion.

The vital quality to have in your drawing is the "spirit" of movement. You cannot be successful as an artist if you remain seated in your chair, nor can your drawings be successful if the figures you draw remain static. Nine times out of ten the picture you are asked to do will call for action. Art buyers love action. It adds zest and pep to your work. A number of prominent artists recently revealed the fact that the "drapey" figures are out as definitely as the First World War "flapper." Ours is an age of action. A model cannot be left to pose herself. You will have to think hard: "What can I do with her to make this drawing sing?"

The solution is not easy, for it is a matter of feeling and interpretation. Today a girl on a magazine cover cannot just be sweet. She must be vital in every sense and doing something besides sitting in front of you and having a portrait painted. She cannot just be holding something; the magazine-cover girl has already held everything from cats and dogs to letters from the boy friend. Let her swim, dive, ski through flying snow. Let her do anything, but don't let her be static.

Pictures have changed, and it may be that the camera and photography have been the cause. This does not mean that a drawing cannot be just as vital as a camera study. Only ten years ago the artist did not fully realize what compelling interest lay in action. He had not seen photographs snapped at one thousandth of a second and never dreamed that he could do this himself. Not only magazine covers but any drawing you do will have added selling power with good action. To make it the right kind of action, you will have to find out what action really is and then study it as you would anatomy, values, or any other branch of drawing.

A word of warning must be added against too much duplication of action. If you are drawing several figures, all walking, unless they are marching soldiers, do not make them all walk alike. Interesting action derives from contrast. All the variety you can achieve is needed. A figure appears to move faster if he is passing a stationary or slow-moving figure.

Important, also, is the handling of mass action: soldiers in battle, race horses grouped together, figures scattering away from some danger. Always pick out one or two as the key figures. Put all you have in these. Then group and mass the rest. If you define the individuals equally, the drawing becomes monotonous. Battle pictures should concentrate on one or two figures in the foreground, the rest becoming subordinated to these. It is safe to handle subjects filled with action in this way, since too much attention to the individuals who make up the mass makes for confusion. A group is more powerful than many units.

There is a trick you must learn in order to capture poses that cannot be otherwise obtained —for example, a falling figure in mid-air. You pose the figure, as you want it, on the floor. Use a flat background, get above the figure with the camera, and shoot down. Place him head first, feet first, or any way you want your model. I once did a swan-dive subject by having the girl lie face up across the seat of a chair, and from the top of a table I used a downward shot. You can take the figure this way and then reverse it. By shooting from a very low viewpoint or a high one, many seemingly impossible action shots may be obtained. They must be skillfully done. The artist can disregard the shadows that fall on his background, but the photographer cannot.

Do a lot of experimenting from imagination, from the model, and with your camera. If you can draw well, that is good. If you can add convincing movement, so much the better.

SNAPSHOTS OF RUNNING POSES

REMEMBER
ARMS MOVE OPPOSITE
TO LEGS. BACK FOOT DOES
NOT LEAVE GROUND UNTIL
FRONT FOOT IS PLANTED.
ARMS PASS HIPS AT SAME
TIME KNEES PASS. HIP IS
HIGHER ON SIDE OF FOOT
CARRYING WEIGHT. KNEE
DROPS ON LEG OFF GROUND.
ACTION IS BEST EXPRESSED
AT EXTREMES OF STRIDE.
ALWAYS TIP LINE OF BAL-
ANCE. MAKE THUMBNAILS
OF THESE AS ABOVE.

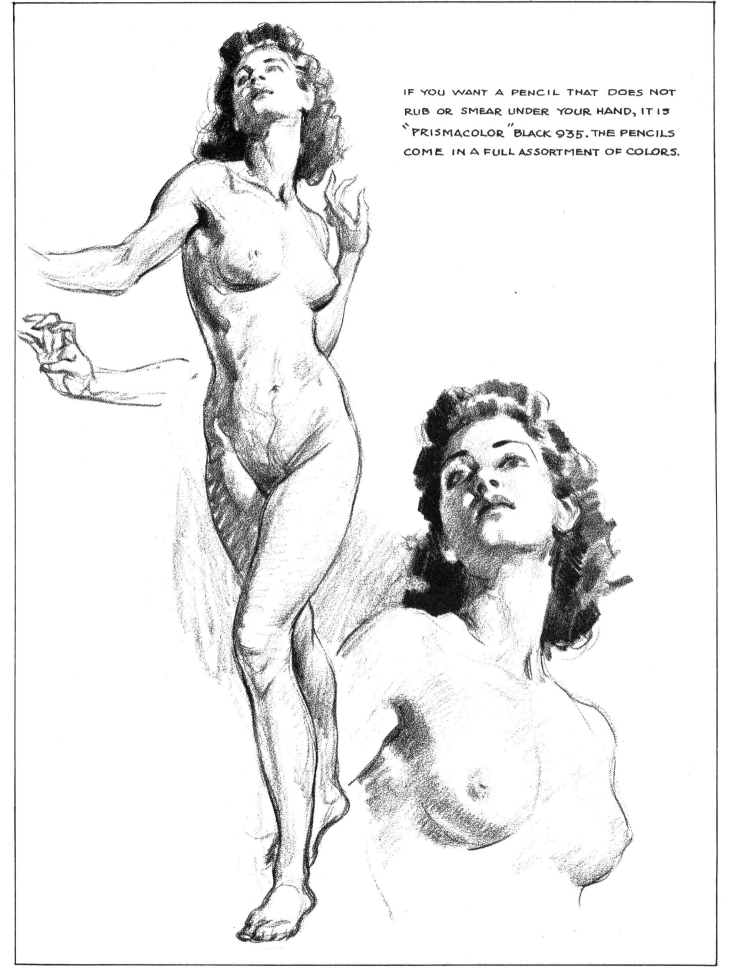

IF YOU WANT A PENCIL THAT DOES NOT RUB OR SMEAR UNDER YOUR HAND, IT IS "PRISMACOLOR" BLACK 935. THE PENCILS COME IN A FULL ASSORTMENT OF COLORS.

A TYPICAL PROBLEM

A typical problem based on the assumption that you are employed by an art service:

You are wanted in the front office.

"Good morning. I've called you in to meet Mr. Saunders. I'd like you to get the information from him firsthand."

Mr. Saunders: "To make this brief, I am organizing a new company for parcel delivery. We are starting out with a fleet of new trucks. All will be painted a bright red. Our name will be, 'Saunders' Snappy Service'; our slogan, 'We'll deliver anything, anytime, anywhere.' We want a trade-mark designed to display prominently on our trucks, in our advertising, and on our stationery. We'd like a figure of some kind within a circle or triangle, or some other odd shape. It ought to be symbolic of speed. You can include any kind of device, such as wings, an arrow—anything that would get across the idea of speed.

Please don't make another winged Mercury. It's been done to death. It can be dignified or clever. We cannot use a messenger-boy device because it is not typical of the company. Our men will wear uniforms and a cap bearing our trade-mark. Please submit some rough ideas in pencil."

Take one or two of your best roughs and finish them in black and white for a line cut. Do not use halftone. Keep them very simple.

Make a flat design in black and one or two other colors for the design to go on the trucks.

Design a small sticker to be pasted on parcels. This will incorporate the trade-mark and the lettering, "Delivered promptly, safely, by Saunders' Snappy Service." Size to reduce to two by three inches.

Design some direct-by-mail postcards for possible use. These should be simple, original, striking.

VIII. BALANCE, RHYTHM, RENDERING

Balance is a physical attribute each of us must possess. If a figure is drawn without balance, it irritates us subconsciously. Our instinct is to set firmly on its base anything that is wobbling and likely to fall. Watch how quickly a mother's hand grasps the teetering child. The observer recognizes quickly that a drawing is out of balance, and his inability to do anything about it sets up a negative response.

Balance is an equalized distribution of weight in the figure as in anything else. If we lean over to one side, an arm or leg is extended on the opposite side to compensate for the unequal distribution of weight over the foot or two feet that are the central point of division for the line of balance. If we stand on one foot, the weight must be distributed much as it is in a spinning top. The figure will then fit into a triangle. If we stand on both feet, we make a square base for the weight, and the figure will then fit into a rectangle.

This should not be taken too literally since an arm or foot may emerge from the triangle or rectangle, but the division line through the middle of the triangle or rectangle will show that there is approximately a like amount of bulk on each side of it.

When you are using a live model either for direct sketching or for camera shots, she will automatically keep in balance—she cannot help it. But in drawing action from the imagination balance must be watched carefully. It is easy to forget.

Before going into the problem of rhythm, the fundamentals of rendering must be taken into account. Suggestions for rendering technically in different mediums will appear throughout the rest of the book. Technique is an individual quality, and no one can positively state that a technical treatment popular or successful today will be so tomorrow. The fundamentals of rendering, however, are not so much concerned with how you put your strokes on paper or canvas as with correct values rendered intelligently for the specified reproduction and a clear conception of the use of tone and line in their proper place.

On page 132 are two drawings that I believe will be self-explanatory. In the first, tone is subordinated to line; in the other, line is subordinated to tone. This gives you two jumping-off places. You can start a drawing with the definite plan of making it either a pure line drawing, a combination of line and tone (in which either can be subordinated to the other), or a purely tonal drawing like the one on page 133. I suggest that you do not confine yourself to a single manner of approach and treat all your work in the same way. Try pen and ink, charcoal, line drawing with a brush, watercolor, or whatever you will. The broader you make your experience in different treatments and mediums, the wider your scope becomes as a practicing artist. If you are making a study, then decide first what you want most from that study. If it is values, then make a careful tonal drawing. If it is construction, line, proportion, or anatomy, work with these in mind. If it is a suggestion for a pose, the quick sketch is better than something labored over. The point is that you will have to labor when you want a detailed or tonal statement. You need not labor quite so hard to express a bit of action. If your client wants a sketch, see that it remains a sketch and that you will have something more in the way of finish to add to your final drawing.

WHEN THE FIGURE STANDS ON ONE FOOT, THE
MAIN WEIGHT IS DISTRIBUTED WITHIN A
TRIANGLE; IF ON BOTH FEET, THEN WITHIN
A RECTANGLE; ABOUT LIKE THE LETTERS
Y AND R

BALANCE IS A MECHANICAL PRINCIPLE
IT AFFECTS EVERY FIGURE

TONE SUBORDINATED TO OUTLINE

HERE ARE TWO APPROACHES WHICH WILL
PRODUCE ENTIRELY DIFFERENT RESULTS.
TRY BOTH. LINE IS REALLY THE FORTE OF
THE DRAUGHTSMAN, WHILE TONE IS THE ALLY
OF THE PAINTER. TONE IS MORE DIFFICULT
AND SHOULD NOT BE "FAKED". THERE CAN BE
MANY HAPPY COMBINATIONS OF BOTH.

OUTLINE SUBORDINATED TO TONE

132

TONAL STUDY

LINE STUDY FOR
CONSTRUCTION

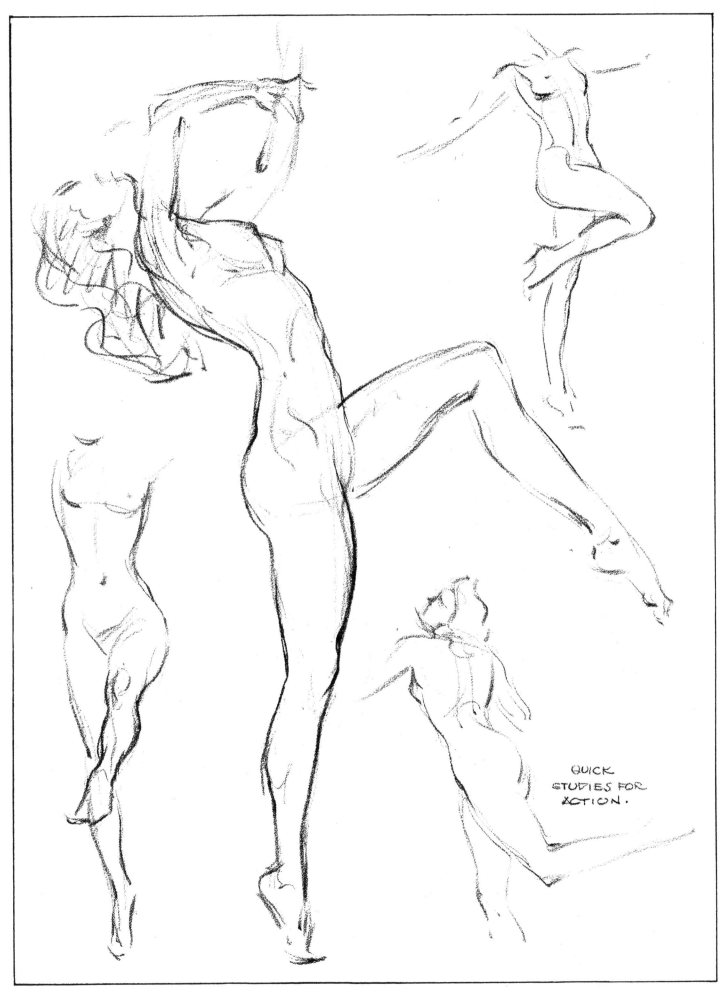

QUICK
STUDIES FOR
ACTION.

BASIC LINES OF RHYTHM

HOGARTH LINE OF BEAUTY

CLASSIC SPIRALS

ARCS

THE PAROBOLA

"S"

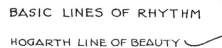

FIG. I

RHYTHM

AXIOM: ANY CONTOUR THAT CAN BE EXTENDED OR MADE TO "FLOW" INTO ANOTHER ADDS UNITY, GRACE AND RHYTHM.

PROCEDURE: SIGHT ALONG A CONTOUR. SEE IF YOU CAN "PICK UP" THE "SWING" OF THE LINE IN ANOTHER CONTOUR WITHOUT DISTORTION OR INCORRECT DRAWING. (FIG I) YOU WILL FIND THE AVERAGE SUBJECT FULL OF RHYTHM IF YOU LOOK FOR IT. KEEP YOUR PENCIL DOWN ON THE PAPER.

RHYTHM

The feeling of rhythm is of tremendous importance in figure drawing. Unfortunately, it is one of the easiest things to miss. In music we feel tempo and rhythm. In drawing it is much the same. Considered technically, rhythm is a "flow" of continuous line resulting in a sense of unity and grace.

We call the rhythmic emphasis on a line or contour "picking up." The line of an edge, observed across the form, will be picked up and continued along another contour. The next few drawings may serve as examples. Look for this phenomenon of rhythmic line, and you will find its beauty in all natural forms — in animals, leaves, grasses, flowers, sea shells, and in the human figure.

We are conscious of the rhythm that pulses through the universe, beginning with the atom and ending with the stars. Rhythm suggests repetition, flow, cycles, waves, and all are related to a unified plan or purpose. The feeling of rhythm in drawing, aside from the abstract, is a "follow-through" in line, just as it is in the movements of various sports. A bowler or golfer, a tennis player, or any other athlete must master the smooth "follow-through" to develop rhythm. Follow your lines through the solid form and watch them become part of a rhythmic plan. When a drawing looks clumsy, the chances are that the trouble lies in its lack of "follow-through." Clumsiness in action—and in drawing —is lack of rhythm that results in a jerky, uneven, disorganized movement.

There are some basic lines of rhythm for which we can be constantly on the alert. The first is called the "Hogarth" line of beauty. It is a line that gracefully curves in one direction and then reverses itself. In the human form, it is present everywhere: in the line of the spine, the upper lip, the ear, the hair, the waist and hips, and down the side of the leg to the ankle. It is like the letter S in variation.

A second line of rhythm is the spiral, a line starting at a point and swinging around that point in a spreading, circular movement. This rhythm of line is apparent in sea shells, a whirlpool, or a pinwheel.

The third line of rhythm is called the parabola, which is a sweep of line continually bending to a greater curve, like the course of a skyrocket. These three lines are the basis of most ornamentation. They can also be made the basis of pictorial composition. They seem to be so thoroughly a part of all graceful movement that they should be given great consideration in all drawing of movement. The lines of rhythm in animals are easily observed and hence easily comprehended.

Rhythm may be forceful, as in great waves beating upon a coast, or gentle and flowing, as in the ripples of a pond. Recurrent rhythm moves and stirs us, or gives us a feeling of restfulness and composure, pleasing to the senses. The so-called "streamline" is rhythm applied to ugly contour. The commercial application of this principle has been eminently successful. The lines of our trains and ships and motorcars, our planes, and our household appliances have been built upon this concept first recognized in nature—in the dolphin among other fish, in birds, and in all living things designed for swift motion.

SHADOWS

LONG LINES

SWING YOUR PENCIL VERY LIGHTLY
AT FIRST. FEEL FOR THE RHYTHM AND
FLOW OF CONTOUR. NEVER MIND IF
YOUR DRAWING SEEMS TO GET GREY
AND "MESSY". BEST TO USE A SHORT
STUB OF A PENCIL, THEN HOLD UNDER
HAND BETWEEN THUMB AND FIRST
FINGER. ADD HEAVY LINES LAST.

DOTTED LINES ARE TO CALL YOUR ATTENTION TO THE WAY CONTOURS MAY BE "WOVEN" TOGETHER ACROSS THE FORM. NO TWO POSES WORK ALIKE BUT WHEN THE CONTOURS HAVE THE "FEELING" OF BEING CONNECTED AND A PART OF EACH OTHER THEN A "SYMPHONY" OF LINE IS ESTABLISHED. RHYTHM IN DRAWING, AS IN MUSIC, UNIFIES THE WHOLE SO THAT THE FEELING AND MOVEMENT OF ALL BECOMES MORE IMPORTANT THAN ANY SINGLE PART. KEEP FEELING FOR THE CORRECT AND EXPRESSIVE LINE. IF IT DOESN'T GO DOWN THE FIRST TIME, BRING ANOTHER LINE DOWN. SOMETIMES A NUMBER OF LINES ARE MORE EXPRESSIVE THAN ONE, LIKE RIPPLES ON WATER REPEATING THE MOVEMENT. RHYTHM CAN LIFT YOUR ABILITY TO THE SKIES.

FIGURE POSED AGAINST A WHITE
BACKGROUND TO DEMONSTRATE
HOW THE FORM MAY BE DEFINED
WITH SINGLE LIGHT, WITHOUT
OBVIOUS USE OF OUTLINE. THE
OUTLINE IS DRAWN VERY LIGHTLY
FOLLOWED BY A CAREFUL STUDY
OF TONE, EDGES AND ACCENTS.

A TYPICAL PROBLEM

A typical problem worked out with an account executive in an advertising agency:

"Your work has come to my attention," says the executive of an advertising agency, "and, from what I have seen of it so far, I like it very much. I have a new gasoline account, for which we must have a fresh approach. I want to use a new man in the field, and he must be good. We will cover all advertising mediums pretty thoroughly, but the initial punch will come from outdoor advertising in a series of bill posters. Whether or not we give you this series to do depends upon what you can show us in the way of art work in roughs and sketches. We are willing to pay five hundred dollars per poster to the right man, this price to include all preliminary work. The name of the product is Sparko Rhythm Motor Fuel. As a starter, here are some captions we have thought up: *Tune Your Motor to Sparko Rhythm; Heard Everywhere…Sparko Rhythm; Sparko Rhythm Sounds Sweet in any Motor; "Swing" to Sparko Rhythm; Always in Step with Sparko Rhythm; Let Your Motor Sing to Sparko Rhythm; In Time, Every Time, That's Sparko Rhythm; Keep in Tune with Sparko Rhythm.* You will note that we are thinking in musical terms, but we will be glad to consider any ideas that associate rhythm with a motor fuel."

The width of an outdoor poster is two-and-a-quarter times the height. Make several small roughs on tissue for ideas that could be used to illustrate the above. You do not have to show an automobile, or a motor, but bear in mind that it is a motor fuel. The words "motor fuel" must be somewhere on the poster. You will probably want to use a base line of lettering across the bottom of the poster: "America's Greatest Motor Fuel." The sheets in a poster run four across, and two and a half up and down. The half-sheet may be placed either at top or bottom. Try to avoid cutting through a face at the joining place of two sheets. If the face is very large, see that the joining places do not cut through the eyes. Sometimes the sheets vary a little in color, and the bill poster cannot be relied upon not to get one sheet pasted a little off.

Work up in color your best ideas in sketch form. Size of poster for sketch is ten by twenty-two and one-half inches. A margin of white goes around the poster about two inches at top and bottom, and three at the sides.

I am not going to suggest what to do, but what not to do, as far as your design is concerned.

Do not make the name Sparko Rhythm too small.

Do not put dark lettering on a dark background.

Do not put light lettering on a light background.

Get some good copy for your style of lettering; don't "originate."

Keep lettering very simple and readable; don't get fancy.

Don't fake your figures; get good copy.

Don't make small figures or too many.

If you would like to experiment, draw or paint the finished poster: the size will be, in inches, sixteen by thirty-six or twenty by forty-five. Paint a white margin at least two inches top and bottom and three or more at sides.

Save your effort as a sample.

IX. THE KNEELING, CROUCHING, SITTING FIGURE

In this chapter we are concerned with qualities other than motion. Almost the whole gamut of feeling can be expressed in a seated figure. It can suggest alertness or composure, fatigue, dejection, aggressiveness, timidity, aloofness, uneasiness, boredom. Each would be expressed differently. Sit down or have someone do so, and see how you would dramatize each of these.

It is of paramount importance, at this point, to understand the shifting of the weight from the feet to the buttocks, thighs, hands, elbows, back, the neck and head. Important, too, is the correct understanding of foreshortened limbs that assume other than usual contours. In such poses limbs become props or braces rather than complete supports. The spine has a tendency to relax in a concave manner toward such bracing. When you are sitting on the floor, one of your arms usually becomes a brace, and the spine relaxes toward the bracing shoulder. One shoulder is high and the other one drops; the hips lean toward the brace; the weight is carried on one side of the buttocks, the side of the supporting arm.

When you are sitting in a chair, your spine may lose its S-shape and become a C. The thighs and buttocks take the weight. Both flatten a good deal, particularly a woman's thighs. The position of the head over the body should be carefully placed, since it has much to do with what the pose suggests. The draftsman must decide whether the sitting pose should be erect or relaxed. Remember that the figure is always subject to the law of gravity. It should have weight, or it cannot be convincing.

Foreshortening will require subtle observation, for no two poses are quite alike. Every pose off the feet will be a new problem and probably one you have not solved before. The variations of viewpoint, lighting, perspective, the unlimited variety of poses, all keep the problems of drawing new and interesting. I cannot think of anything less animated or more boring to look at or to draw than a model who is "just sitting." This, to me, means both feet close together on the floor, arms resting alike on the arms of the chair, back flat against the chair, eyes looking straight ahead. Your model might half-turn toward you, hang an arm over the back of the chair, cross her feet, stretch them out, or hold a knee. Use plenty of imagination to change a dull pose into an interesting one.

Let the whole pose of the model as well as the hands and facial expression tell the story. Do you want her to show animation or weariness? If she sits at a table, talking to her fiancé, let her lean forward, absorbedly, or show displeasure if they are quarreling.

Watch carefully for contours arranged in front of each other and draw them that way; if you do not, a thigh will not recede, a part of an arm will look too short or stumplike. Remember that if the hands or feet are close to the camera, they photograph too large. Any figure that is quite foreshortened should be photographed from a distance if possible, and then enlarged for copy. If you are planning a portrait, find a natural gesture or pose for your sitter. Turn the chair at an odd angle, get an unusual viewpoint, don't have the head stiffly above the neck. Let her drop comfortably into the corner of the chair, feet drawn back or even drawn under her, or feet extended and knees crossed. Don't let the legs make a perfect right angle with the knees.

You must stir yourself on to invention.

IT SHOULD BE REPEATED OVER AND OVER TO THE
STUDENT NOT TO "FAKE" LIGHT AND SHADOW ON
THE FIGURE. DRAW FROM THE MODEL OR FROM A
GOOD PHOTO. FIVE MINUTES OF "SEEING" IS
WORTH DAYS OF FAKING. SHADOWS CAN BE SEEN
FLATTER AND SIMPLER THAN THEY ARE.

DENCIL POINT RENDERINGS

ABOVE : VERTICAL LINE MODELING

RIGHT : A PENLIKE TREATMENT

A PEN TREATMENT PLANNED IN
PENCIL SAVES TIME AND TROUBLE.

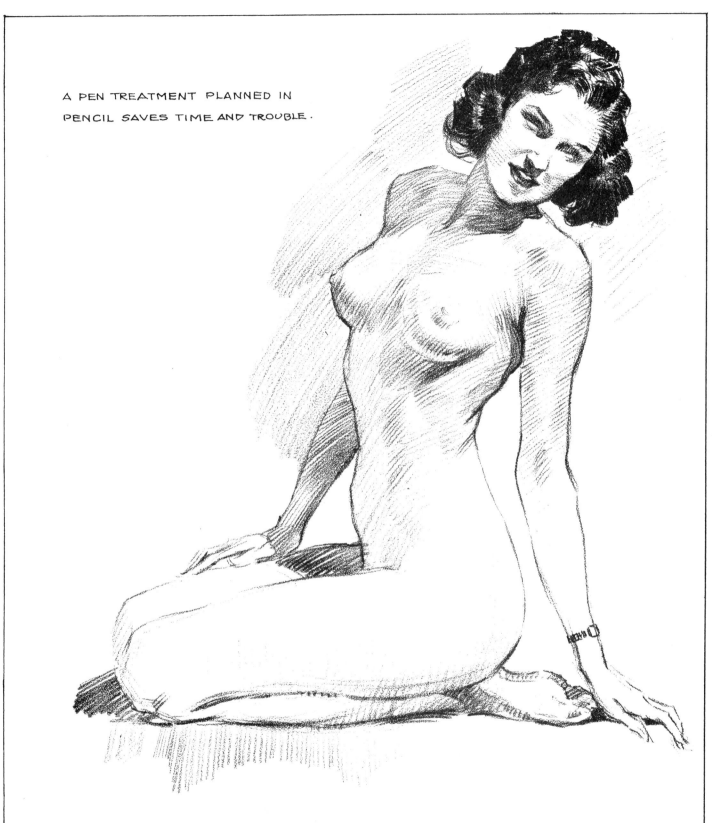

MODELING WITH THE PENCIL POINT IS SLOWER AND MORE DIFFICULT. IT IS
ALSO MORE LIMITED AS TO TONE VALUES. HOWEVER IT SHOULD BE OFTEN
PRACTICED TO DEVELOP THE KNACK OF PEN DRAWING.

A COMBINATION OF BLACK AND GRADED TONE OFFERS UNIQUE POSSIBILITIES. DRAWING WAS DONE ON "BAINBRIDGE COQUILLE NO.2". THE BLACKS ARE HIGGINS INK. THE TONES ARE DONE WITH "PRISMACOLOR" BLACK 935 PENCIL. REDUCTION IS ONE THIRD.

AN EXAMPLE OF LINE DRAWING AND PENCIL IN COMBINATION. DRAWN ON BAINBRIDGE COQUILLE NO 3, WITH A FINE POINTED SABLE BRUSH AND HIGGINS AMERICAN INDIA INK. A WASH COULD BE USED WITH THIS INK.

PEN DRAWING

PEN AND INK STUDIES

THE STROKES PLANNED WITH A SHARP
PENCIL, INKED IN, AND DRAWING CLEANED
WITH KNEADED ERASER. IT IS A GOOD
PLAN TO "FOLLOW THE DIRECTION OF
THE PLANE OR FORM," WITH THE STROKES.

PEN SKETCHING

FORGET YOURSELF, YOUR
PEN AND YOUR STROKES.
LOOK FOR RHYTHM, MASS,
ACTION. NOBODY EXPECTS
A SKETCH TO BE COMPLETE.

DRAWN WITH A SMALL CAMELS HAIR BRUSH AND DRAWING INK ON BRISTOL BOARD

A TYPICAL PROBLEM

A number of typical problems in a contest for sculptural designs:

1. The problem is to design a group of figures for a large fountain to be placed in the center of a circular pool fifty feet in diameter. The subject is, "I am America. I give thee liberty and a free life." The drawings are to be submitted for interpretation of idea only. The group may contain a heroic figure symbolizing the Goddess of Liberty. The work should be American in spirit. Figures can typify agriculture, mining, industrial life, the home, et cetera. The artist, however, is not limited in any way.

2. Design a large drinking fountain. Somewhere upon the base will be the inscription: "I am America. From my lakes and streams I give thee the waters of freedom."

3. Design a sun dial to be placed within the botanical gardens, bearing the following inscription: "I am America. I give thee my soil."

4. Design a statue for the zoological gardens, the inscription to be: "I am America. I give all living things the right to life."

5. Design a soldiers' and sailors' monument. The inscription to read: "I am America. These of my sons I gave for thy security."

Here are unlimited opportunities to express yourself. One interesting manner of handling these designs, after having worked out rough tissue sketches, would be to draw on toned paper with charcoal and white chalk. In these there would be considerable study of the figure, action, drapery, dramatic interpretation. Work out your ideas with your pencil, your camera, material gathered by research, et cetera.

There is no objection to using allegorical or semi-nude figures, but do not stick too close to the Greek. Make it American.

X. THE RECLINING FIGURE

One of the most challenging phases of figure drawing is that of the reclining pose. It offers the best opportunity of all for design, interesting pose, pattern, and foreshortening. We forget the body as an upright figure for the moment and think of it as a means of flexible pattern for space-filling. The head may be placed anywhere within the space at your disposal. The torso may be regarded from any viewpoint. In the drawing of the reclining figure, as in the standing and sitting poses, avoid straight, uninteresting poses —the legs straight, the arms straight, the head straight. I call these "coffin poses," for nothing appears quite so dead. Unlimited variety is possible with the reclining or half-reclining poses. We brought the figure out of the "proportion box" early in this book. Never fit a box around anything that is an interpretation of life.

The impression is that reclining poses are extremely difficult to draw. If you are accustomed to measuring off so many heads, you must discard the method in drawing the reclining figure, for it may be foreshortened to so great an extent that it cannot be measured in heads. But there is still height and width in any pose. You can still find the middle and quarter points and make comparative measurements. From here to there is equal to from there to another point. Measurements are not standard and apply only to the subject before you.

Reclining poses are often neglected in art schools. The reason is usually the crowded room in which one student obstructs the view of another. Consequently the most delightful and interesting phase of figure drawing is passed over, and many students leave the school without the slightest idea of how to go about drawing a reclining figure.

The appearance of complete relaxation is of first importance. A stiff-looking pose gives the observer the reaction of discomfort. The rhythm of the pose should be sought very carefully. You know now how to look for it. Almost any model looks better in a reclining than in a standing pose. The reason is that the stomach falls inward and appears more slender; the breasts, if inclined to droop, return to normal roundness; the chest becomes full and high; the back, lying flat, is straighter; even a double chin is lost. Perhaps nature purposely adds beauty to the reclining pose. If glamorous appeal is needed in a drawing, nothing can give it more than the reclining figure.

If you are using your camera, do not place it too close to the model, for distortion will result. Reclining poses should be selected with good taste. Crudity can send you and your drawing out the door in a hurry. See that the pose does not hide parts of the limbs so that they look like stumps; for instance, a leg bent under with nothing to explain it may look like the fellow with the tin cup. You cannot tell whether or not he has a leg. An unusual pose is not necessarily good, but a figure can be twisted about for interesting design, or combined with draperies for unusual pattern. The hair can be made a nice part of the design. If the pose is complex, keep the lighting simple. Cross-lighting on an unfamiliar pose may complicate it and make it look like a Chinese puzzle. If bizarre effects, however, are wanted, it may work out at that. A high viewpoint may lend variety.

STUDY IN FORESHORTENING

THE DRAWINGS ON THESE TWO PAGES ARE
INTENDED TO DEMONSTRATE HOW THE
TEXTURE OR "GRAIN" OF THE PAPER MAY BE
UTILIZED TO ADVANTAGE. THE DELICATE
MODELING IS DONE WITH THE POINT AND
THE BROADER MASSES WITH THE SIDE OF
THE LEAD. ATTENTION IS CALLED TO THE USE
OF DARK ACCENTS. YOU CANNOT "INVENT" LIGHT
AND SHADOW. DRAW FROM LIFE OR GOOD COPY.

Typical problem to solve with an art dealer and representative:

"I have a particular commission in mind that I believe you could handle," says an art dealer. "My clients have organized a new country club. They are building a beautiful clubhouse. They want two mural decorations for their new dining room. The woodwork will be done in ivory, with a slightly deeper tone of ivory on the walls. There are two doorways into the dining room, over each of which there will be a lunette. The lunettes are half-circles, the radius of each being five feet, making the base or span of the mural ten feet, five feet in height at the middle point. The club is to be closed between the months of October and May for the winter, and, since the club activities start in May, a spring mural will be used over one door and a fall subject over the other.

"The subject selected for the first lunette is awakening spring. A reclining figure lies upon the woodland soil, amid wildflowers that have burst into bloom, blossoming bushes, and trees. There are small animals about, such as squirrel, deer, rabbit, and birds. The figure is in the act of awakening and about to rise. Her hair is long, and perhaps there is a garland of early spring flowers about her head. The figure may be partly covered with flowers.

"A female figure lying down to rest for the winter is the fall subject. Brilliant autumn leaves are falling and have drifted over the figure, cov-ering it partly. In the hair are drooping and wilted flowers. A squirrel with an acorn in its paws, a rabbit burrowing down into the soil, birds flying—all may be shown. The grass is brown and dry; perhaps some red berries are on a branch. The thought that is conveyed is that summer has ended and Nature prepares for winter."

Make many rough pencil compositions. Do not only fill the space with the figure stretched stiffly across it. Proceed to work up some small thumbnail roughs in color. Then pose your model, make studies, or take camera shots. It would be wise to make some studies of trees and foliage in the woods. The little animals should also be studied. The subject could be given modern, simple treatment. When your preliminary material is ready, begin the sketch you will submit. This sketch is called a cartoon. It should be done well enough so that it can be squared off. You may then work from it, if necessary, directly upon the walls, or on a canvas mounted to fit or to be glued into place.

Since the room is light and airy, the paintings should be keyed fairly high, rather than dark and heavy. Gray your colors a little so that your picture will not jump out of the wall like an advertisement. Treat the flesh delicately and simply. Do not try for brilliant or even strong light and shadow. You will gain valuable experience if you will paint these subjects on a small scale.

XI. THE HEAD, HANDS, AND FEET

The head, perhaps, has more to do with selling a drawing than anything else. Though the figure drawing you submit may be a splendid one, your client will not look beyond a homely or badly drawn face. I have often worried and labored over this fact in my own experience. Once something happened that has helped me ever since. I discovered *construction*. I discovered that a beautiful face is not necessarily a type. It is not hair, color, eyes, nose, or mouth. Any set of features in a skull that is normal can be made into a face that is interesting and arresting, if not actually beautiful. When the face on your drawing is ugly and seems to leer at you, forget the features and look to the construction and placement of them. No face can be out of construction and look right or beautiful. There must be a positive balance of the two sides of the face. The spacing between the eyes must be right in relation to the skull. The perspective or viewpoint of the face must be consistent with the skull also. The placement of the ear must be accurate, or a rather imbecilic look results. The hairline is extremely important because it not only frames the head but helps to tip the face at its proper angle.

The placement of the mouth at its proper distance between nose and chin can mean the difference between allure and a disgruntled pout. To summarize, draw the skull correctly from your viewpoint and then place the features properly within it.

In my first book, *Fun with a Pencil,* I set about to work out a plan for head construction that I consider almost foolproof. I repeat the general plan as a possible aid here.*

---

*A strikingly similar method was originated independently by Miss E. Grace Hanks. (See *Fun with a Pencil,* p. 36.)

Consider the head a ball, flattened at the sides, to which the facial plane is attached. The plane is divided into three equal parts (lines *A*, *B*, and *C*). The ball itself is divided in half. Line *A* becomes the earline, *B* the middle line of the face, and *C* the line of the brows. The spacing of the features can then be laid out on these lines. The plan holds good for either male or female, the difference being in the more bony structure, the heavier brows, the larger mouth in the male. The jaw line in the male is usually drawn more squarely and ruggedly.

In this chapter are studies of the skull and its bony structure, as well as the muscular construction and the general planes of the male head. The individual features are worked out in detail. The heads are of varying ages. Since no two faces are alike, for you the best plan is to draw people rather than stock heads. Perhaps an artist of another era could repeat his types endlessly, but there is no advantage in that today. It tends to make an artist's work dated in short order. The artist who can keep his types fresh and true to purpose will last.

It pays in the long run to hire models, though there is always the temptation to save money. The danger in using clips from magazines is that the material is usually copyrighted. Advertisers pay movie stars for the privilege of using their photos. Both the star and the advertiser will resent having them "swiped" for another advertiser. Your client will not be happy about it either. The same is true of fashion models who have been paid for their services. You cannot expect to use them for your own purposes. Practice from clips, but don't try to sell your copies as originals. Once you learn to draw heads, it will be your life-long interest to portray character.

HEAD BUILDING

HOW TO CONSTRUCT A HEAD.

DRAW A BALL. DIVIDE BALL INTO SECTIONS SO THAT YOU HAVE A MIDDLE LINE
DIVIDING BALL 3 WAYS (LINES A, B AND C). TAKE ONE FOR MIDDLE LINE OF FACE. THE
OTHER TWO WILL BE AN EAR LINE AND A LINE OF BROWS. DROP MIDDLE LINE OF FACE
OFF BALL. DIVIDE INTO 4 PARTS THAT APPEAR EQUAL, EACH PART EQUAL TO HALF OF
THE DISTANCE FROM BROWLINE TO TOP OF BALL. SLICE OFF SIDES BY DROPPING EAR
LINE STRAIGHT DOWN. PLACE EAR AT INTERSECTION OF LINES A AND C. NOW BUILD IN JAW
AND FEATURES. THIS PLAN IS MORE THOROUGHLY COVERED IN "FUN WITH A PENCIL".

THE SIMPLE FORM DEVELOPED TO THE COMPLEX, THROUGH THE USE OF PLANES.
THESE AVERAGE PLANES SHOULD BE LEARNED. THEY ARE THE BASIS FOR LIGHTING.

THE PLANES SIDE VIEW. GET SOME CLAY AND MODEL THE PLANES SO YOU CAN
LIGHT THEM DIFFERENT WAYS. THEN DRAW THEM. REFER BACK TO PAGES 72 AND 73.

BACK VIEWS ARE MOST DIFFICULT UNLESS FORM AND PLANES ARE UNDERSTOOD.

GRUESOME! BUT TRY TO DRAW IT CAREFULLY.

1 FRONTALIS	5 MASSETER	10 BUCCINATOR
2 ORBICULARIS OCULI	6-7 ZYGOMATICUS	11 DEPRESSOR
3 AURICULAR MUSCLES	8 ORBICULARIS ORIS	12 STERNO MASTOID
4 TEMPORALIS (DEEP)	9 TRIANGULARIS	13 TRAPEZIUS

STUDIES OF AN ANATOMICAL CAST (WHITE)

THESE ARE TO SHOW THE ANATOMY OF
THE HEAD IN ITS SOLID ASPECT, OR AS FORM
IN LIGHT AND SHADOW. IF YOU CAN DRAW
FROM CASTS, IT IS RECOMMENDED TO DO
SO. MANY STUDENTS SKIP THE ANTIQUE
CLASS, NOT REALIZING ITS TRUE VALUE.
IT'S ADVANTAGE IS THAT THE SUBJECT
REMAINS FIXED FOR CAREFUL STUDY. IT
DEVELOPS SOLIDITY AND EXCELLENT
FOR STUDY OF VALUES. I SUGGEST YOU
MAKE SOME CAREFUL FREEHAND
DUPLICATIONS OF THESE DRAWINGS
IF YOU HAVE NO SIMILAR CASTS NEAR.

DRAWN FROM PHOTO RELEASED EXCLUSIVELY TO ANDREW LOOMIS, CANNOT BE COPIED FOR COMMERCIAL PURPOSES.

STUDIES OF A YOUNG MAN

THERE ARE NO SECRETS IN DRAW-
ING HEADS. FIRST COMES AN UN-
DERSTANDING OF A PARTICULAR
SKULL. NEXT TO CONSTRUCT AN
INDIVIDUAL SET OF FEATURES
CORRECTLY PLACED WITHIN
THAT SKULL. THEN COMES THE
RENDERING OF THE FORM OVER
THE FACE BY PLANES OF LIGHT
HALFTONE AND SHADOW. EVERY
PLANE IS A PART OF THE WHOLE
THE LIGHTING SHOULD BE VERY
SIMPLE. THE HEAD IS DIFFICULT
ENOUGH WITHOUT ADDING THE
COMPLEXITY OF MANY LIGHTS.

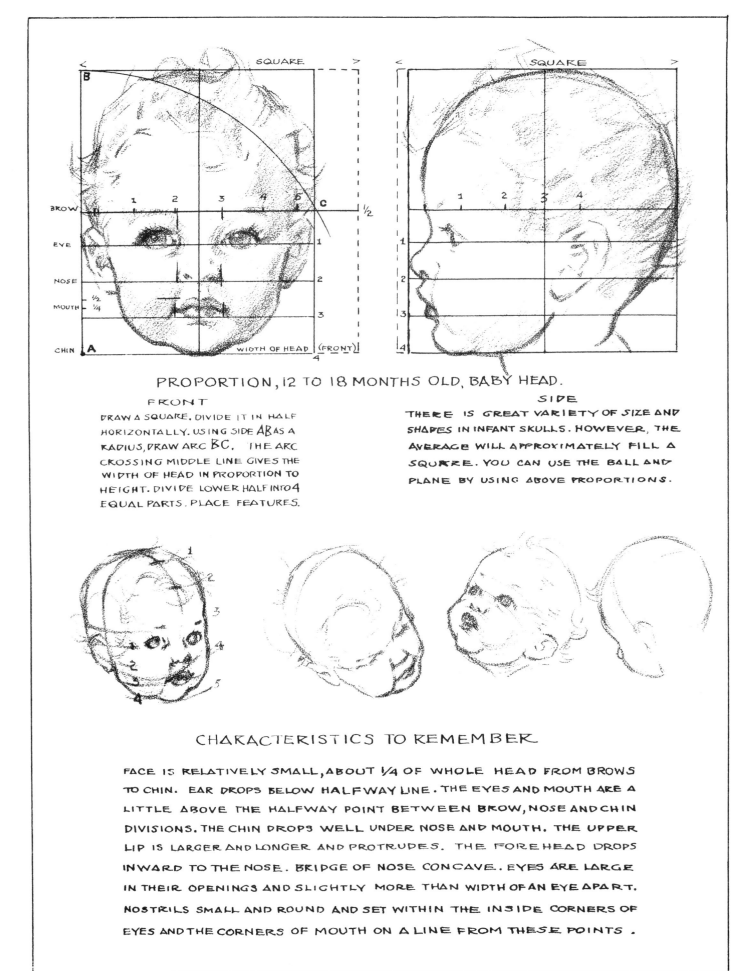

PROPORTION, 12 TO 18 MONTHS OLD, BABY HEAD.

FRONT

DRAW A SQUARE. DIVIDE IT IN HALF HORIZONTALLY. USING SIDE AB AS A RADIUS, DRAW ARC BC. THE ARC CROSSING MIDDLE LINE GIVES THE WIDTH OF HEAD IN PROPORTION TO HEIGHT. DIVIDE LOWER HALF INTO 4 EQUAL PARTS. PLACE FEATURES.

SIDE

THERE IS GREAT VARIETY OF SIZE AND SHAPES IN INFANT SKULLS. HOWEVER, THE AVERAGE WILL APPROXIMATELY FILL A SQUARE. YOU CAN USE THE BALL AND PLANE BY USING ABOVE PROPORTIONS.

CHARACTERISTICS TO REMEMBER

FACE IS RELATIVELY SMALL, ABOUT 1/4 OF WHOLE HEAD FROM BROWS TO CHIN. EAR DROPS BELOW HALFWAY LINE. THE EYES AND MOUTH ARE A LITTLE ABOVE THE HALFWAY POINT BETWEEN BROW, NOSE AND CHIN DIVISIONS. THE CHIN DROPS WELL UNDER NOSE AND MOUTH. THE UPPER LIP IS LARGER AND LONGER AND PROTRUDES. THE FOREHEAD DROPS INWARD TO THE NOSE. BRIDGE OF NOSE CONCAVE. EYES ARE LARGE IN THEIR OPENINGS AND SLIGHTLY MORE THAN WIDTH OF AN EYE APART. NOSTRILS SMALL AND ROUND AND SET WITHIN THE INSIDE CORNERS OF EYES AND THE CORNERS OF MOUTH ON A LINE FROM THESE POINTS .

HANDS

LEFT HAND FRONT AND BACK

MIDDLE FINGER LONGEST

3RD FINGER
1ST FINGER

4TH FINGER

THUMB

X POSITION OF KNUCKLES IN RELATION TO PALM

DRAW FINGERS SEPARATELY UNTIL YOU CAN BEND THEM IN ANY DIRECTION.

DRAW AT LEAST ONE HAND DAILY FROM LIFE OR GOOD COPY

THERE IS NO MYSTERY IN THE METHOD OF DRAWING HANDS. IT IS A MATTER OF FITTING PIECES TOGETHER PROPORTIONATELY. BLOCK IN THE APPROXIMATE AREA OF THE WHOLE HAND, FITTING EACH PART AS IT APPEARS. THE LENGTH OF THE HAND IS ABOUT EQUAL TO THE FACE FROM HAIRLINE TO BOTTOM OF CHIN. WATCH CAREFULLY CONTOURS PASSING IN FRONT OF EACH OTHER: THE PALM IS CONCAVE, THE BACK CONVEX. KEEP AT IT!

THE FOOT

IT IS SUGGESTED THAT YOU DRAW YOUR OWN FEET
IN MANY POSES, SETTING A MIRROR ON THE FLOOR.
ALSO, THAT YOU SET UP SHOES AND DRAW THEM FROM
MANY ANGLES AND VIEWPOINTS.

A TYPICAL PROBLEM

A typical problem outlined by an art buyer:

"We always need artists who can draw heads well. Good drawings of heads are required in almost all advertising, for illustrations on magazine covers, and litho displays. An acceptable head must be in good drawing, to be sure, but that's only the beginning of its job. If it's a pretty girl's head, the pose, the animation, the hair-do, the costume, the color, the type, the expression, the age, the idea behind it, all count. For character drawing, I shall expect you to find a living type to work from, for the sake of authenticity, and, if necessary, add whatever particularized qualities the job specifies. I cannot tell you what to do or how to paint it. Do the necessary work, bring it in, and, if I like it, I'll buy it. That's the only way our firm buys art work. When you have convinced me that you can do a good head, I may give you further commissions, but I must reserve the right to reject any work and may even ask you to redraw a job."

Begin with a magazine cover and experiment until you have arrived at a good idea. Work it out small, in color, until you feel the little sketch has carrying power and attention value. Then work up your final drawing. Keep it as simple as possible. Don't try to sell a faked, or "cribbed," head. No magazine will buy it. Do not send work to a magazine that already employs one artist regularly, since he is probably working under contract.

Other suggestions are: Make a number of studies of the people around you. Draw yourself in the mirror. Draw a baby, a child, a young man and girl, a middle-aged person of each sex, and an old person of each sex also. Spend most of your time drawing heads—your market demands them.

XII. THE COMPLETE FIGURE IN COSTUME

Costumes will keep changing, but the human figure remains the same. You must know the form beneath the folds of the clothing. You must familiarize yourself with the methods of cutting flat material and fitting it over the rounded figure. The drape of the material is caused by the manner in which it is cut and joined. Material cut on the bias drapes differently from that cut on the weave. Try to understand what makes the material do what it does in the ruffle, the pleat, the flounce, and in gathering; what is the purpose of a dart; and why the seams and joinings cause the flat material to shape itself. You do not have to know how to sew, but you must look for the construction of the clothing, just as you look for the structure of the figure under it. It takes only a few extra minutes to find out which folds are due to the construction of the garment and which are caused by the underlying form. Find the "intention" of the drape. Discover what the designer has worked for—slimness or fullness. If a seam is smooth, it was intended to lie flat. If there is a shirring or gathering at some point, take note that it was *not* intended to lie flat. You must not slavishly copy each tiny fold, but neither must you disregard folds entirely. Indicate the shirring at that point.

Learn how the female figure affects the folds: the fabric falls away from the most prominent forms underneath shoulders, breasts, hips, buttocks, and knees. When material is loosely draped over these, the folds start with them and radiate to the next high point. When the material is fitted, if there are any folds at all, the folds will run around the prominent forms, pulling at the seams. The male form molds the clothes in a like manner. In a man's suit, for example, the material over the shoulders, over the chest, and over the top of the back is cut to fit. The only folds you find then come from the pull at the seams. The bottom of the coat and the trousers are draped loosely. The trouser folds radiate from the buttocks to the knee in sitting poses and from the knee to the calf and the back of the ankle.

An overmodeled garment is just as bad as an overmodeled figure. Watch to see that your light and dark values stay within the color value of the material itself and that its unity is not broken by lights and shadows that are more strongly stated than necessary.

Do not draw every seam, every fold, and every button, but try to understand constructive principles and interpret them correctly in what you do put down, instead of being careless in these matters or remaining totally ignorant of them.

No matter what you draw—figure, costume, furniture—learn its construction, so that you *can* draw it.

2/3

3/4

1/2

1/4

KNOW YOUR FIGURE UNDER THE COSTUME

AN EXCELLENT METHOD FOR PRACTICE NOW IS TO TAKE FASHION PHOTOS TO WORK FROM, AND, AS INDICATED ABOVE, DRAW BOTH COSTUME AND FIGURE UNDERNEATH, AS IF CLOTHING WERE TRANSPARENT. YOU WILL UNDERSTAND THEN THE RELATIONSHIP OF THE DRAPE TO THE FORM UNDERNEATH. YOU MUST BE ABLE TO RECONSTRUCT A CLOTHED FIGURE.

THE RENDERING OF DRAPERY IS SO COMPLICATED AT BEST, THAT ONLY A VERY SKILLED ARTISAN COULD ANTICIPATE WHAT DRAPERY WILL DO IN A GIVEN INSTANCE, UNDER CERTAIN LIGHT AND WITH CERTAIN TEXTURE. "FAKED" CLOTHING USUALLY LOOKS IT, AND WILL NOT SELL THE AVERAGE ART BUYER. MAKE IT A RULE ··· RIGHT NOW!

RENDERING OF DRAPERY IS AN ARTICULATION OF PLANES ARRANGED IN PROPER VALUES.

STUDY FOR A STORY ILLUSTRATION. HERE IS A TYPICAL PROCEDURE OF DRAWING HALFTONES AND SHADOWS ONLY, LEAVING LIGHTS WHITE.

STUDY FOR STORY ILLUSTRATION.
HERE A BACK LIGHTING PROVED
EFFECTIVE FOR A VIGNETTE.

STUDY FOR AN ADVERTISEMENT

The problem of equipping yourself to do your job well:

What is the next step? you may inquire.

Look about at the kinds of work you see displayed everywhere. What kind of work do you want to do? Once you make up your mind, practice that kind of drawing with brush or pencil. You are going to need mental equipment as well as skill with your hand. Try to know more about your subject than the other fellow. Remember you can borrow only a little; most of your knowledge must come from your own observation, your determination, and your plain courage.

Find a way that you can allow yourself one, two, three, or even four hours a day for drawing. Next, supply yourself with materials and a place to work. Keep a fresh sheet of paper on your drawing board at all times with other materials at hand.

Hunt for subjects that interest you. Note them down and pin the notes to your board. If you can do nothing better, set up an interesting still life and work from it until you have learned something from it.

Start a portfolio of samples of your best work. Don't take out a drawing and throw it away until you have a better one with which to replace it. When you have a dozen good drawings, show them. Don't wait for an expensive collection.

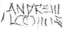

DRAWN WITH A SOFT PENCIL ON
BRISTOL BOARD. DRAWING IS
RUBBED WITH FINGER OR A
PAPER STUMP. HIGHLIGHTS
ARE PICKED OUT WITH KNEADED
RUBBER. MANY ARTISTS LIKE
THE WIDER RANGE OF VALUES
AFFORDED BY THIS METHOD. SPRAY
WITH FIXATIVE. GOOD LUCK!

CLOSING CHAT

There is always a hesitation before turning in a finished job. It occurs to me as I complete this book, and it will occur to you when you look over a piece of your work: Could it not have been done better? It may seem to you that you should have used a different approach, or a better method of construction. My own philosophy is to do the best I am capable of within the time requirements, and then to make the decision that the drawing is now finished and must be turned in. Lack of decision is a harmful thing. You can learn by your mistake and make amends, but the energy must go into a fresh effort.

Learn to use time wisely. You will not always have the time to do a drawing twice or three times in order to select the best example. While you are a student, use precious hours to the best advantage. A bit of anatomy misunderstood in an important job that must go tonight, a problem in perspective that remains unsolved, ruins a painting on which you have spent days and paid expensive models' fees.

When, early in your career, an art director asks you to re-do a drawing, be grateful that you are granted the time. It is a tragedy when your drawing ought to be done over and cannot be for lack of time. You deliver something you do not like, and the publisher is forced to accept it. He is generous if he gives you another job.

The term "talent" needs clarifying. To any man who has slaved to acquire skill in his art, it is most irritating to have his ability referred to as a "gift." Perhaps there is one genius in a hundred years or more who can achieve perfection by "divine inspiration." I have never met such a man, and I do not know any successful artist who did not get there by the sweat of his brow. Again, I do not know of a single successful artist who does not continue to work hard.

There is no formula in art that will not break down as soon as the effort behind it ceases. But, to compensate, there is no reward on earth that can compare with a pat on the back for a hard job well done. Talent, in its underclothes, is a capacity for a certain kind of learning. Talent is an urge, an insatiable desire to excel, coupled with indefatigable powers of concentration and production. Talent and ability are like sunlight and a truck garden. The sun must be there to begin with, but, added to it, there must be plowing, planting, weeding, hoeing, destroying of parasites—all have to be done before your garden will yield produce. According to those one-inch ads we see so often, you can be an artist, play the piano, write a book, be compelling, convince anybody, make friends, and get a high-salaried job if you'll just sit down and answer it—and, of course, "kick in."

If you want to draw, if you want to gamble all your chips for stakes that are really worth while, you have an excellent chance of winning. If you just dabble, you will certainly lose your ante, for the others in the game are playing their hands for all they are worth. I have met students who have said they would like to learn drawing as a "sideline." There are no sidelines. You are either in the game or out of it. "Well, then, how do I know I'm going to be good enough to make a go of it?" No one can possibly be assured that he is going to be good enough at anything to make a go of it. Faith in yourself and industry are all that any of us have got to go on.

An honest book on drawing can only point the way and suggest procedure. A book of downright promise can be nothing but downright fake. It is natural for young men and women to look for the "secrets" that allegedly assure success. It is even reasonable to feel that these secrets are somewhere hidden away, and that to reveal them would assure success. I confess I thought so myself at one time. But there are no such secrets, jealously guarded by the older generation so that it need not give way to the younger. There is not a craft in all the world that opens its doors so wide to the young and lays its knowledge so freely at its feet. Note that I say knowledge, for all the secrets are knowledge. Everything about this craft is fundamental. Expert use of the fundamentals is the only basis there is for learning to draw. These fundamentals can be listed, studied, and carried out in your own way. They are: proportion, anatomy, perspective, values, color, and knowledge of mediums and materials. Each of these can be the subject of infinite study and observation. If there is a secret, it is only in your individual expression.

The artist obtains his work in different ways, depending on the branch of the craft in which he specializes:

In an advertising agency there is usually a creative or art department. Here the layouts or visualizations are made. There is a copy writer, an account executive, and a layout man who together have planned an individual ad or a whole campaign. An appropriation has been made by the advertiser. The magazine space has been decided upon and contracted for. As the ideas are worked out, in sketch or layout form, they are submitted to the client and O.K.'d or rejected. It has been decided that either photographic or art work shall be used. All this has taken place before you are called in. By this time, a closing date has been set, and it is usually not far off, since the preparatory work has taken a good deal of time.

You are handed the layout as O.K.'d or with instructions for changes. Most agencies give you considerable leeway for pictorial interpretation, but your drawing must fit the space in the layout. If you are working with an art organization, you will not see the agency at all, but will get your instructions and the agency layout from one of your company's salesmen.

Proceed, then, to look up what data you need, get necessary photos or models, and go ahead with your job. If you are a free-lance artist, you work in your own studio. In that case you will have agreed upon a price with the art director, and you will bill the agency when the job is complete and accepted. In an art organization you will either be working at a set salary, or on a split basis, usually fifty-fifty. Most artists spend considerable time in organizations before setting up a free-lance studio.

The magazine illustrator usually works in his own studio. He may have an agent or sales representative, especially if he does not live in New York City, where most of the magazine houses are located. Without an agent he deals directly with the art director. The artist is handed a manuscript. As a general rule, if the magazine has not supplied him with layouts, he is asked to make roughs for general composition and treatment of the subject. The magazine may pick the situation to illustrate or may ask the artist to read it, pick the situations, and submit several roughs for selection. When these are O.K.'d, the artist proceeds with his drawings. When the magazine picks the situation and gives the artist a rough from the art department, he may go to work at once. This is usually the most satisfactory arrangement, but it does not give the artist so much freedom as when he makes his own selection. If you have an agent, the agent bills the work; otherwise you are paid directly. An agent's commission is approximately twenty-five per cent of the billing price. There are several firms and guilds in New York that act as artists' agents. Work must be of proven quality, however, before they will represent an artist.

Outdoor posters are handled through advertising agencies or through lithographers. The artist seldom deals directly with the advertiser. There are also outdoor advertising companies that buy art work and in turn sell it to the advertiser. In the latter case the lithographer is called in on a competitive basis.

Newspaper drawing may be done in art organizations, by the paper's staff, by the advertiser's own department, or in the free-lancer's own studio. Displays are done in the lithographer's art departments or are bought from organizations or free-lance artists.

Magazine covers are usually speculative. You simply make them, send them in, and most of the time you get them back. You are expected to send return postage or express charges. Sometimes you can send in a preliminary sketch. If the magazine is interested, you may be asked to make a final drawing or painting, but the art editor reserves the right to reject it unless you are so well known in the field and so dependable that you can be relied upon to bring in an acceptable cover design.

Comics are handled speculatively, as are magazine covers, except in the case of newspapers. There they generally come through feature syndicates. In this case you work on a salary or royalty basis, or both. You must have several months of your feature completed on a strip before your work will be considered. Sometimes royalty is paid by the comic magazine or syndicate, in addition to the purchase of first serial rights.

First-rate advertising may pay more than story illustration. Methods of reproduction are so accurate today that almost anything painted or drawn may be reproduced with fidelity. Knowing these methods is valuable information. Most engraving houses are glad to show their equipment and methods to the artist. They know that if he understands their problem, he can help them by producing clean copy. This is also true of lithographers. It is important to remember that a newspaper uses line or coarse-screen halftone. Pulp magazines must use a coarser screen than other magazines. This means keeping fairly contrasting values to assure good reproduction. In all halftone reproduction the whites of your subject gray down somewhat; the middle tones flatten a little; and the darks become somewhat lighter. Watercolor is about the best medium for reproduction since it has no shine, is usually made small, and therefore requires less reduction. Any of the drawing mediums, however, can be reproduced well. Never submit a drawing on flimsy paper.

The artist should, early in his career, form the habit of orderliness. Keep things where you can find them. Your drawing, when submitted, should be scrupulously clean and matted with a flap to protect it from dirt. Keep your file in order and clip whatever you think will make it as complete in information as possible. I have a method of filing that works out nicely: I make an index in alphabetical order of what I have filed and then give my folders consecutive numbers. In this way I put several subjects in one file. For instance, I list bedrooms under *B*, and the file number for this subject is put alongside the listing. I also list sleeping poses under *S* and give it the same number. My folders go from one to three hundred. I can add as many more as I wish or add more subjects within the present folders by simply listing the additional subjects alphabetically and assigning a folder number. I have gradually learned the folder numbers, and, as soon as I see a subject, I find it without referring to the index. For instance, I know that airplanes go in number sixty-seven. On every clipping I jot down the file number and put the clip into the drawer that contains the number. I have filled seven filing cabinet drawers. I can now go directly to a file that contains a school classroom by looking it up alphabetically under S and getting the file number. Without a filing system, hours upon hours can be lost looking through hundreds of clippings to find a single one. It is a good investment for the artist to subscribe to a number of magazines. By keeping your copies in order, they eventually become valuable. For instance, if I should need material to illustrate a story laid in 1931, I could go back to the styles worn in that period without difficulty. Or to interiors. Or to the automobile that the characters owned. Some day you may want to know what they were wearing during the Second World War. What were the soldiers' helmets like? The magazines are brimming over with that material now. When the war is history, it will be hard to find.

Develop an orderly procedure in your work. Get the habit of making small studies before you start something big. Your problems will appear in the sketches and can be worked out then, so that you will not be stumped later on. If you are not going to like a color scheme, find it out before you have put in days of work. I remember a poster I once painted. When I was through, I began to wonder how a different color background would have looked. When I had put the second background on, it looked worse. By the time I had tried about six, I was resigned to going back to the first. It was all lost motion that could have been avoided by making thumbnail sketches first. I could have done several posters in the time wasted, and my work would not have lost its original freshness.

If you once decide on a pose, stick to it. Don't let yourself muddy up a subject by wondering if the arm might not have been better some other way. If you must change it, start over and so keep it fresh. The more clearly you have a drawing defined in your mind and in the preliminary sketches, the better the result will be. Many drawings will have to be changed to please your clients. The changes are often unreasonable and are matters of opinion, but do not grumble, at least aloud. A chronic grumbler is an unpopular fellow, and soon the jobs go to the man who seems to be more cheerful, especially if his work is equally good. Again, enthusiasm and cheerfulness add their own qualities to your work. Robert Henri said, "Every stroke reflects the mood of the artist at the moment." He is confident or hesitant, happy or somber, certain or perplexed. You cannot hide mood in a creative work.

On the subject of prices, it is better in your early years to get your work published and circulated than to quibble over price. The more you get published, the better known you become. The better known you are, the more work you get. The more work you get, the better will be your price. Eventually you find your price level, since you can keep raising your price as long as more people want your work than you can supply. If nobody will pay the price you are asking or if you cannot keep busy at your prices, you'd better come down. It's just plain business.

I admit you are apt to run into a buyer who will take advantage of your youth or your lack of work, but, if you are capable, his very use of your work may boost you clear out of his class. There is no way to place a value on a piece of your work. The chances are that you will get a fair deal from a reputable client. If you do not, it won't be long before you will discover it. You will soon find out if you are asking too much. Posters can go all the way up the ladder from fifty dollars to one thousand. Magazine illustrations range from ten or twenty to five hundred or more a picture. The purpose, the client, the artistic merit—all these influence the price.

Attend an art school if you can, but carefully consider the instructors. If you can get a man to teach you who is active in his field, well and good. Ask for the names of some of his former pupils. If the school can show a convincing list of professional men who were formerly his students, fine. If not, hunt up another school.

Let me make a suggestion or two about the preparation of an artist's samples. There is slight possibility of being accepted as a professional artist without a well-executed group of samples. I have urged throughout this book that you retain the best of your practice work for samples. Do not limit yourself to my problems alone. If you want to do figure work, prepare your samples for that purpose. Do not submit nudes, however, since there is no possibility of their being used. The excellence of your figure drawing, however, should be present in your costume drawing. Submit one or two girl subjects, perhaps a man, or a man and a girl. A child subject is always of value. Keep your subjects on the happy side for advertising, and don't forget glamour appeal.

All of the foregoing also holds true for story illustration, although magazines are interested in characterization, action, and drama as well. If you want to do posters, your approach must be different, since here simplicity is of first importance. Do not mix up your presentation, by which I mean that you should not submit a drawing obviously designed for a poster or advertising illustration to a magazine editor of fiction. Try to fit your presentation to your client's needs. Don't submit a great raft of drawings. An art director can see from your first two or three samples what he can expect of you. He is a busy fellow. He will keep looking as long as your subjects, treatments, and mediums are varied, if they are at all good. If he looks at twenty drawings, he is just being polite. Don't impose on the man.

A very good method of introducing yourself is to make up small packets of photographic copies of your samples. These may be mailed to many prospective clients, together with your address and telephone number. Interested people will get in touch with you. I followed this scheme when I set up my own studio after working for several years in various art organizations. I photographed proofs of the work I had done for or through the organizations. The result proved well worth the expense. Many new customers were brought to light.

It is advisable to start a library. There are many good books on art: anatomy, perspective, the work of the old masters, and modern art. Buy all you can afford. Read art magazines. Many valuable suggestions will come to you this way.

Although I have emphasized the figure, part of your time should be devoted to other subjects for drawing. Draw animals, still-life subjects, furniture, interiors, or whatever else is likely to be an accessory to the figure. Outdoor sketching and painting is wonderful for training your eye to color and value as well as form.

Painting will help your drawing, and vice versa. The two are so interrelated that they should not be thought of as distinct and separate. You can paint with a pencil and draw with a brush.

For color practice, use some of the color photography you find in the magazines to render in oil or water color. Pastel is a delightful medium for practice. There are many kinds of color crayons and pencils with which to experiment.

It is a constant challenge of the profession that you never know what you will be called upon to do next. It may be anything from a lemon pie to a Madonna. As long as it has light falling upon it, color, and form, it can be made interesting. I recall an advertising campaign some years ago for so prosaic a subject as enameled kitchenware. But what the artist made of it was exquisite. I recall the Henry Maust water colors that advertised hams and foodstuffs. They were as beautifully executed as any fine English water color.

Simple things such as a few garden vegetables, a vase of cut flowers, an old barn, present all the problems there are to master. Each of these may be a vehicle for your individual expression. Each can be so beautiful as to be worthy of a place in a fine arts gallery. That is the scope of things to be seen, felt, and set down. Clouds were there for Turner; they are here for you and will be here for your great-grandson. The qualities of light on flesh are present for you as they were for Velasquez, and you have as much right to express yourself as he had, and much less superstition and prejudice to combat. You can set up the almost identical pan of apples with which Cézanne gave a lasting message to the art world.

You can look for yourself at the haze of atmosphere that entranced Corot or the burst of late-afternoon light that enthralled Innes. Art will never die—it just awaits eyes to see and hands and brain to interpret. The paintable waves will not cease breaking with Frederick Waugh, nor will pictures be forgotten with the continuing rise of radio. You will also have materials never dreamed of, subjects that we cannot now imagine. You will have new purposes for art that have never before existed. I believe the human body has been increasing in beauty, although it is hardly discernible to us. Think of how standards change, for example, and of a modern girl beside a buxom maid of Rubens' time. It would be a little hard to imagine one of his beauties walking down Main Street in slacks. I doubt whether his favorite model could get to the judges' stand in one of our innumerable beauty contests.

All the things have not been done in art that can and will be done. I don't think our bones and muscles will change much and that light will shine differently, so all the good rules will still hold. I can only say that you must have the courage of your convictions, believing that your way is right for you and for your time. Your individuality will always be your precious right and must be treasured. Take from the rest of us all that you can assimilate, that can become a part of you, but never still the small voice that whispers to you, "I like it better my way."